BORN AGAIN *and* BEYOND

BORN AGAIN
and BEYOND

John E. Harvey

CASCADE *Books* • Eugene, Oregon

BORN AGAIN AND BEYOND

Copyright © 2014 John E. Harvey. All rights reserved. Except for brief quotations in critical publications or reviews, no part of this book may be reproduced in any manner without prior written permission from the publisher. Write: Permissions, Wipf and Stock Publishers, 199 W. 8th Ave., Suite 3, Eugene, OR 97401.

Cascade Books
An Imprint of Wipf and Stock Publishers
199 W. 8th Ave., Suite 3
Eugene, OR 97401

www.wipfandstock.com

ISBN 13: 978-1-62032-740-1

Cataloging-in-Publication data:

John E. Harvey.

Born again and beyond / John E. Harvey.

x + 122 p.; 23 cm—

ISBN 13: 978-1-62032-740-1

1. Evangelicalism. 2. Bible—Hermeneutics. 3. Theology—Methodology—History. I. Title.

BR1642 H7 2014

Manufactured in the USA.

All scripture quotations, unless otherwise indicated, are taken from the Holy Bible, New International Version®, NIV®. Copyright ©1973, 1978, 1984, 2011 by Biblica, Inc.™ Used by permission of Zondervan. All rights reserved worldwide. www.zondervan.com The "NIV" and "New International Version" are trademarks registered in the United States Patent and Trademark Office by Biblica, Inc.™

For Natalie and Daniella
treasures from Jesus

Table of Contents

Preface ix

Introduction: A Good Place to Start 1

Chapter One: Truth and the Bible 7

Chapter Two: The Authority of the Bible 25

Chapter Three: Knowing and Doctrine 48

Chapter Four: The Gospel and the Cross 69

Chapter Five: Salvation and Spirituality 91

Chapter Six: All Truth Is God's Truth 108

Conclusion: Evangelicalism on the Edge 119

List of Illustrations

The Story of the Bible as a Chiasm 42
The Knowing-Doing-Being Triad 48
Interdependence of the Knowing-Doing-Being Triad 49

Preface

I ORIGINALLY THOUGHT OF writing this book sometime in the late 1990s. Had I put pen to paper at that time, though, the book might have been more aptly named *Beyond Born Again* rather than *Born Again and Beyond*, as my disregard for Evangelicalism was still untamed. I was rather angry. But as subsequent years unfolded, I grew to having a greater ease with Evangelicalism. I now conclude that while there are many features of Evangelicalism that are in dire need of adjustment, and while it takes itself too seriously, there is really no need for me to be upset about its oversights or its rather presumptuous claim to be the principal vehicle of God's truth in this world. The simple fact is that such presumption is really no different than the high regard that most religious cultures have of themselves. One would be hard-pressed to find any religious culture that did not in some way presuppose that it is somehow representative of the divine mind (even those religious cultures that express theological generosity to other expressions of faith maintain that their generosity is a reflection of the divine mind). Evangelicalism is what it is: a conservative Protestant expression of the Christian faith. As such, it is but one of many expressions of Christian faith. It would therefore be to my advantage to glean those fruitful elements from it that I can—even as I consider delightful emphases in other expressions of Christian faith.

My journey from anger to acceptance has been most costly, for during this journey I caused hurt and disillusionment to many people. This did not happen while I lived and taught in Africa. First, because the theological questions that confronted me there were very different from the ones that I brought with me. Second, if ever a stray word came from my mouth my Nigerian students would simply categorize it as being yet another peculiarity of white folk. But this has not always been the case for me in various North American settings—a Roman Catholic seminary, a Christian Reformed

Preface

university, a Baptist church, or even the little Anglican church of which I am now (most happily) a minister. My fear is that at times I have been more an instrument of doubt than of faith. All the same, I am easy on myself, for the pain that I have gone through has enabled me to help others process inner turmoil regarding their experience with Evangelicalism. To my great delight, I can think of several people who have found God even while they were expressing heart-felt angst about Evangelicalism.

I have many people to thank. I thank my wife, Suzanne, and my children, Natalie and Daniella, for their patience and support. I thank my friend and colleague, Bob Derrenbacker, for commenting on an earlier draft of this work and for his many helpful suggestions. I thank my church community, which has given me the time needed to write this book. I also thank the many people who have shared their perspectives and stories with me—sometimes with despair and disillusionment, sometimes with hope and conviction, but always with great honesty.

Introduction: A Good Place to Start

THIS BOOK IS ULTIMATELY about the spiritual life. Although it concerns various subjects pertaining to Christian belief and practice, its predominant concern is life in God. The principal idea of this book is that while Evangelicalism has much to offer the world, it is needlessly hampered by erroneous assumptions concerning knowledge, the Bible, and salvation. I am not writing this book as an outsider who is looking in, or as a wolf in sheep's clothing. My every word stems from years of soul searching, discerning, and longing for the health of Christ's church within the context of Evangelicalism.

I grew up in a good home, but a home with no religious instruction. My first recollection of things divine was when I was a Cub Scout, perhaps when I was six or seven. My Cub pack met in the vestibule of a church prior to setting off on an outdoor excursion. Out of curiosity, I opened the doors to the church proper. As I looked into the dim room with its stained glass windows, choir loft and pulpit, I was overcome by a sense of awe. Years later I remember talking to my grandfather about God and the afterlife. I guess that I must have been rather dismissive, as Grandpa chastised me for my disregard. When I was fourteen the God-question was once again at the forefront of my mind, for in that year both my grandfather and a close friend died. I can remember praying for them even in their death. I prayed that things would go well for them in the afterlife. I am not sure why I did so as I had not received any religious education to that point. I began to think that maybe I should somehow align myself with God—whoever God was.

When I was sixteen I became smitten by a pretty girl who happened to be a Jehovah's Witness. Her faith did not concern me at all. Like many teenage boys, I was initially enthralled with more mundane matters. Yet it was not such matters that proved to captivate me. Elders of the Kingdom Hall that I was attending told my girlfriend that she needed to choose either me or the Kingdom Hall. She chose the Kingdom Hall, and I found myself in a teenage depression. I remember walking through the stubble of a recently harvested field on a beautiful moonlit night. I cried out to God something like the following, "I have nowhere else to turn but to you. Save me from my grief. I give myself to you." If I had to mark a moment in time that I turned to God, it would be then. My turning to God had a life-giving influence in my life. My interests, concerns, and lifestyle changed dramatically—to the amazement (and chagrin) of some of my schoolmates.

My enthusiasm for God led me to a Christian college, where for four years I studied the Bible together with various liberal arts. While I was at college I learned about and embraced various tenets of Evangelicalism. After college I became a pastor of a Baptist church, and although I pursued the cause of Evangelicalism with much vim and vigor, I must say that there was angst in my heart. The tenets of the Baptist faith did not seem to give me the tranquility of soul for which I longed. As I look back at my experiences in college and as a Baptist minister, I clearly see that I did not distinguish between my religious sub-culture (Evangelicalism) and the Christian faith. The two were, in my mind, one and the same.

Following my experience as a Baptist minister, I moved on to a Masters degree. I thought that the institution was safe, for while it subscribed to the Evangelical faith it also sought to expose students to other understandings of the Christian tradition. It was largely due to such openness that I began to question Evangelicalism's understanding of the nature of Scripture, the cross, and conversion. My experience at this institution was bittersweet: sweet, insofar as the longing that I had for tranquility of soul began to be met as I explored the spiritual quest outside the confines of Evangelicalism; and bitter insofar as my naiveté concerning the nature of Scripture began to unwind. Such bitterness was not simply academic, for the Evangelical understanding of the Christian faith stands or falls on its particular understanding of the nature of Scripture.

The unravelling of Evangelicalism that had begun years earlier was furthered with my PhD in Old Testament. Doing such a PhD interested me not because I wanted to become a professor or because I sought to situate myself in the academic community, but because doing so might help me to attain a more satisfying understanding of the Christian faith. Whereas the Masters degree safely introduced me to some of the problems inherent in

Introduction: A Good Place to Start

the Evangelical understanding of the nature of Scripture, this final degree overturned several of those Evangelical tenets that I had held to so dearly. Maintaining that the message of Scripture was wholly consistent within itself had become indefensible, even incredible. Various authors and editors of the Old Testament differed from one another; what was approved in one century was anathema in the next; and many of the stories have, at best, a germ of historicity to them. I came upon such conclusions with great hesitancy, care, and even remorse—because I knew that doing so was to reject what I had, until that time, believed was central to the faith. My gradual turn to a heterodox understanding of Scripture (in the eyes of Evangelicalism, that is) was altogether unwilling. I wanted to stay within the Evangelical sub-culture, and I therefore defended an Evangelical viewpoint at every turn. But more than wanting to stay within the Evangelical fold, I wanted to be honest. My overriding concern was integrity and truth, however painful it might be.

I brought this angst of soul with me to rural Nigeria where I was first an instructor, and later the president, of a Baptist seminary. My time in Nigeria was delightful, certainly a high point in my life. I found great satisfaction with assisting my community in economic and educational endeavours. I thoroughly loved doing whatever I could for my people to make their lot in life better—whether it was raising chickens, making a road, or starting a school for the children. The questions and concerns that so beset me concerning the nature of Scripture had taken a back seat for the time being. But not long after returning to Canada and visiting supporting churches, the theological concerns were again before me. The North American variety of Evangelicalism simply cannot exist without its particular understanding of the nature of Scripture. I wanted to continue to be a missionary for the Baptist church, but more than this I wanted to have integrity before God. To return to Nigeria by the economic generosity of the Baptist church was, in my mind, most unethical. After months of equivocating, I made the painful decision that we (my wife, daughter, and myself) would not be returning to Nigeria. For the health of my soul, I now see that I needed to be challenged by what I had learned in university settings, I needed the life-giving experience in Nigeria, and, sadly, I needed to decide not to return to Nigeria—thereby beginning to break from Evangelicalism.

It might be helpful to begin with a definition of Evangelicalism. Evangelicalism is a conservative, Protestant movement that originated in modern times and emphasizes the authority of the Bible, the cross, and conversion.

3

Evangelicalism is to be distinguished from Christian fundamentalism, which typically holds such doctrines in a more aggressive manner. While the term Evangelicalism is derived from the Greek word *euangellion*, which means "good news" or "gospel," Evangelicalism is not thereby to be equated with the gospel. Whereas Evangelicalism is a religious sub-culture that finds its roots in various awakenings, revivals, and missionary movements, the gospel itself is embraced by conservative and liberal Protestants alike, and the gospel found a home in the various Eastern and Western branches of the church many centuries before the birth of Evangelicalism.

It would be a great mistake on my part ever to assume that Evangelicalism is entirely homogenous. Evangelicalism in Europe differs in some respects to Evangelicalism in North America; and within North American Evangelicalism there are many differences. Given that such diversity is equally present in all sub-cultures (whether they are religious, political, ethnic or social), one should not be surprised at this. As I comment on Evangelicalism I will do my best to keep its diversity in mind—it would be irresponsible and unfair not to do so.

Supposing that God's revelation of the truth of Jesus Christ is limited to one tradition or another is wrong-headed, even silly. The truth of Jesus Christ can no more be limited to one perspective or another than the Pacific can be contained in one's teacup. The gospel has been expressed in a myriad of ways by diverse cultures over the last two millennia. Evangelicalism represents but one such expression of the gospel. No doubt, there is much to be loved about Evangelicalism as it has made tremendous contributions to the church and to the world. As such, Evangelicalism can provide a wonderful place to start in the Christian faith. But this is far from saying that Evangelicalism is somehow closest to gospel truth, or that all Christian traditions may be judged by the degree to which they are consistent with Evangelicalism. As with every Christian movement through history, Evangelicalism has had its high points and low points. Certainly a high point includes the advancement of the gospel throughout the world; and a low point has been its scant influence in the world of scholarship—even Biblical scholarship. Equating Evangelicalism with the gospel is thus very dangerous. A common sentiment among Evangelicals, nevertheless, is that the gospel is best represented by the Evangelical faith. But as I hope to demonstrate in this book, there are very real problems with this view.

Setting aside the question of the relationship between the gospel and Evangelicalism for a time, we would do well to revisit the teaching that

Introduction: A Good Place to Start

Evangelicalism is little more than a sub-culture. There is no problem with this, for every human claim to universal truth is, ironically, limited to expressing itself through the lens of a given human perspective. I say "ironically" because the claim to have knowledge of the infinite, the absolute, or the divine can only be known through what is finite, relative, and human. Whereas Christendom may be referred to as a culture, Evangelicalism may be referred to as a sub-culture. Christendom claims that it has knowledge of absolute truth in the life, death, and resurrection of Jesus Christ. Evangelicalism goes further than this by asserting that its particular understanding of the faith is precisely that of the gospel. But such an assertion is dangerous as it ties the gospel to a human tradition. When that human tradition falls short of expectations, the one who embraces it cannot help but question the validity of the gospel itself. I have known many who had been immersed in Evangelicalism for years, only to rid themselves of it upon becoming disappointed with it for one reason or another. This departure from Evangelicalism is not what distresses me. My concern is that all too many people who have left Evangelicalism have unwittingly assumed that their departure was actually a departure from God. This is a terrible mistake. Their friends, their family, their church leaders—even the literature that they read and the music that they enjoyed—together reinforced the assumption that Evangelicalism and the gospel were one and the same. When the given Evangelical reads or hears about something that challenges or undermines the tenets of their sub-culture, they are naturally inclined to think that the faith itself is being threatened. But when we remember that Evangelicalism is but one expression of the gospel, this inclination is altogether unnecessary. There are strengths and weaknesses in every sub-culture, so we err when we assume that a threat to Evangelicalism is a threat to the gospel itself. (Indeed, some of the criticisms in this book could equally be applied to several other sub-cultures in Christendom.)

In this book I will challenge central teachings of Evangelicalism: its perspective on the nature of Scripture, its understanding of redemption, and its view on conversion. I am not thereby seeking to overturn the Evangelical belief system. I simply want to rescue it from the perilous heights that it has needlessly ascended. In chapter 1 I discuss how Evangelicalism bought into a particular understanding of the nature of truth, and how it has imposed this understanding on its understanding of the nature of the Bible. In chapter 2 I address Evangelicalism's understanding of the authority of the Bible, and I outline how such an understanding is problematic in several ways. In chapters 3 through 5 I focus on other doctrinal distinctives of Evangelicalism—such as the nature of the gospel, salvation, and conversion. In chapter 6 I discuss the subject of the relationship between Christianity and other religions.

Chapter One

Truth and the Bible

IN THE COURSE OF teaching theological students, the subject of truth invariably arises. Students are prone to ask, "Is the Bible true?" Before answering this question, I like to probe precisely what they mean by "true." Doing so is neither a semantic game nor an effort to dodge an important question. It marks, rather, an attempt to unmask fraudulent understandings of the nature of truth. Throughout this chapter I will address the question "Is the Bible true?" But before doing so it is important to clarify what the term "true" means.

Part of what it means to be human is to try to understand reality. This can only be done through the lens of who we are, for it is not as if any of us has an untainted objectivity—God's-eye view of things. A common assumption, for instance, is that we inherit traits from family members. The proverb "like father, like son" underlies this conviction. While some of us might spend years trying to show ourselves that this proverb does not apply to us, as we age we nevertheless conclude that one or more rather unsavory traits have indeed passed their way down the family line. (Thankfully, we might also observe how a lovely trait has made its way down to us!) We simply cannot understand ourselves without having some understanding of those features that have been passed onto us from our families.

Again, if you were born in the twentieth century, your set of assumptions may well include a basic understanding of various advances in technology and science. Because you have lived in the affluent West, you may likewise assume that there is a correspondence between prosperity and happiness. Such matters as our gender, our personal tastes, our life experiences, our psychological predispositions, and our education similarly have vital roles to play in shaping the way in which we look at reality. The simple fact is that we can only see and understand any aspect of the created world from where we stand—whether that be our race, our age, the place in which we have lived, or even ourselves. The technical term for the set of assumptions that we hold is "worldview," which is an amalgam of presuppositions that we consciously or subconsciously hold about the basic make-up of our world. By "presuppositions" I am referring to assumptions that everyone has. Assumptions are as integral to the human life as is the air that we breathe: whether we have impressive IQs, or whether we are newborn babies, we all have assumptions about the basic make-up of reality. Such assumptions may be true, partially true, or entirely false. We may hold them consciously or subconsciously, consistently or inconsistently.

We all see things through the lens of our worldviews. This cannot be escaped. There are many factors that shape our worldviews. Differences between how men and women think are suggestive of the fact that the genders often understand things differently. (Men are indeed from Mars even as women are from Venus!) Age is also a determining factor. A well-known joke testifies to this: "My parents were unreasonable when I was a teenager; but just after my teen-years I learned that they had become wise." It is often contended that the older we get, the more balanced we tend to become. As we age our youthful ideals may mature, they may be reshaped, or they may even be overturned. The level and nature of our education also shapes our worldview. The more education that we have, the more liberal we tend to become. Again, if our education is in engineering, we may be more inclined to emphasize the mechanics of how things function than if our education is in the fine arts. Our life experiences also play a part in shaping our worldviews. If we have experienced suffering, abuse, poverty, or other such painful realities, our perspective on things will be shaped accordingly. More generally, the stories, national myths, and religious views that we most identify with will shape our understanding of reality—be it the nature of history, the basis of ethical decision making, or our understanding of knowledge.

Putting things less abstractly, we might think of how a traffic accident might be interpreted or explained by different witnesses. Should there be a doctor at the scene, she might emphasize and define in her mind the physical distress that one of the drivers is experiencing. A minister at the scene might be confronted with such questions as "Why was the driver in such a hurry anyhow?" or "How is this experience going to influence the driver's understanding of life?" The natural interpretation of a police officer might be that of ascertaining who was at fault. So also, a car salesman might wonder if the vehicles will be repaired, or if he would be helping either of the drivers purchase a vehicle in the near future. The list, of course, could go on and on. We can only understand reality through the lens of our individuality.

Differing worldviews often exacerbate arguments between people (or even nations). I am reminded of a conversation that I had with a geology student who spent his summers in the bush researching the movement of mountains. His sister joined him one summer, and he recounted how one afternoon a bear entered their camp and brutally mauled her. I naturally suggested that the next time that he went he might bring a gun. It was clear from the geologist's response that he was aghast at my suggestion: "It would be unethical for me to shoot a bear; I am in its territory after all." It was equally difficult for me to comprehend that the geologist would sooner be mauled than shoot an offending bear. The fact is that our conclusions were formed on the basis of very different worldviews. Whereas my ethic was based on the assumption that the needs of a person are more important than those of an animal, the geologist's ethic was based on the assumption that people and animals are completely equal.

A highly influential component of any worldview is cultural setting. One's views on most everything are shaped, even sometimes determined, by cultural mores. When I lived in Nigeria I remember telling my seminary students that if I ever caught any of them drinking beer, I would immediately expel them. (In reality I would not have done so, but as a "big man" in that society I needed to present myself in a no-nonsense manner.) In the same breath I told my students that one of the first things that I was going to do upon returning to Canada was have a beer with my friends in a pub. While the only purpose for drinking beer in that part of Nigeria was to get drunk, drinking a beer at a pub with friends in Canada is, for me, all about having fun with friends. (Indeed, becoming intoxicated in this Canadian context is shameful.) I said this to my students (as we were discussing the ethics of Corinthians eating food sacrificed to idols) because I sought to emphasize that living the gospel may express itself in very different ways in different cultural contexts. Context is everything. This example may be innocent enough; yet all too many believers do not reflect on the profound influence that a culture might have in shaping their understanding of the Christian faith.

We here turn from the effect that culture in general may have on understanding the faith to how religious culture itself shapes faith. In a most naïve manner, we often think that there is no separation between the truth of God in Jesus and the expression of this good news in one's religio-cultural setting—be it North American Pentecostalism, African Roman Catholicism, or anything else in between. But the fact of the matter is that the particular religious setting can even determine how the good news is understood, such that one may conclude that the truest (or only!) expression of the good news is found in one's religious setting. Such a narrow understanding places people in spiritually toxic situations.

I have met all too many Evangelicals who, when confronted with different ways of looking at things that challenge or even undermine the views of Evangelicalism, have discarded the faith altogether—rather than concluding that something might be problematic with Evangelicalism, or their denomination, or their church. While I understand and appreciate the need to defend the faith, I have a very real problem with tying Christian faith so closely to one or another expression—for when the expression is called into question, some people are apt to call the whole faith into question. When, for instance, a fundamentalist Christian learns what scientists have concluded about the universe, the shift of tectonic plates, or the fossil record, such a Christian may well feel compelled to abandon a fundamentalist perspective—and because this person knows no other alternative, they abandon the Christian faith itself. So also, when an Evangelical seminarian learns that there are many life-giving expressions of religious devotion outside the Christian faith, because they have been taught for decades that there is only one legitimate expression of faith, they lose heart. In both instances, and countless others besides, the problem is not with the good news, but the way in which the good news is packaged in one religious culture or another. This holds true for every expression of the good news, certainly not just the Evangelical expression. When the fundamentalist Roman Catholic learns of historical facts that force him to take Roman Catholicism less seriously, this Roman Catholic may have a crisis of faith. When the conservative Lutheran reads of charges that Martin Luther was anti-Semitic, this may place the given Lutheran's faith on a precipice. When the five-point Presbyterian learns that the Westminster Confession of Faith may be overly rational, this Presbyterian may question the gospel itself. When the high-church

Anglican learns of manipulative attempts in the past to suppress other expressions of Christian faith by the state church, such a person may well jettison their own understanding of the good news. It is essential to know that while the good news itself is absolute, the expression of this good news is as varied and rich as is human thought, culture, and experience.

Having discussed the place that worldviews have in shaping our understanding of reality, let us return to a discussion of truth. Common among many people is the assumption that only that which can be historically, mathematically, or scientifically verified is true. This is a very limited understanding of truth, in part because it makes human (and Western) rationality the basis of truth; but this is painfully anthropocentric. Another problem with such an understanding of truth is that it does not take into account the non-physical worlds of ethics and beauty. The statement that the slaughters of Stalin, Hitler, Pol Pot, or Idi Amin were grossly unethical is universally held as being true. Yet the statement cannot be verified historically, mathematically, or scientifically. One can no more prove that such atrocities were evil than one can prove that a particular sunset or view is beautiful. Truth must not be limited to that which can be historically, mathematically, or scientifically verified, for truth greatly transcends rationality.

The assumption that truth is confined to history and science was especially made popular during the eighteenth-century Enlightenment in Europe. The Enlightenment prized human reason, and asserted that religious claims and beliefs are superstitious. Enlightenment mentality continued to flourish in the nineteenth and twentieth centuries, and although postmodernism (which has little regard for human reason, and asserts that there are no absolutes) has blunted many of the excesses of Enlightenment thinking, elements of Enlightenment assumptions concerning truth thrive to this day. Evangelicalism unwittingly adopted Enlightenment assumptions concerning human reasoning. Perhaps it did so because, like other movements, it sought to legitimize itself in the eyes of society. The Western world contended that something is true if it can be supported by history and science. Partly in order to find approval from the world, Evangelicalism therefore embraced Enlightenment thinking.

Evangelicalism's adoption of Enlightenment thinking may be seen in various personages and publications. Certainly one of the most significant Evangelical thinkers of the twentieth century was Carl Henry, a prolific author and editor. Henry emphasized the rational basis for Evangelical faith. Whether it was challenging another worldview or "liberal"

Christianity, Henry vigorously defended the contention that the tenets of Evangelicalism are intellectually solid. In his six-volume theology entitled *God, Revelation, and Authority*, Henry contended that the Evangelical understanding of the faith is more rational than any other understanding. As with Enlightenment thinking, Henry simply assumed that truth is subject to human reasoning. Later in the twentieth century, Campus Crusade for Christ published a now-famous tract called "The Four Spiritual Laws." That its presentation of the gospel is framed by Enlightenment concerns is immediately apparent from the introduction: *"Just as there are physical laws that govern the physical universe,* so are there spiritual laws that govern your relationship with God" (emphasis mine). The phrase "physical laws that govern the universe" is a certain (though probably, accidental) allusion to the three laws of motion that celebrated scientist Isaac Newton proposed in the eighteenth century. That the gospel is to be understood along the lines of a scientific cause-and-effect process is implicit in the tract's outline of "the four spiritual *laws*." According to the tract, salvation is the product of a cognitive process that leads to faith. Altogether absent are such themes as wonder, mystery, and hope—themes that are central to the gospel. To be sure, elements of Evangelicalism have not bought into the Enlightenment project so carelessly. There have been many and diverse movements and people who have had less regard for human reason: some have emphasized the role of conscience and faith; others have concerned themselves with worship and the Holy Spirit; and still others have looked to experience in the discernment of truth. But this cannot be said for Evangelicalism as a whole. Together with much of society, Evangelicalism has found a home in Enlightenment assumptions concerning the nature of truth, and it has sought to explain and understand Christian faith along strictly rational lines.

But Enlightenment assumptions must not be so freely entertained, for they fly in the face of Scripture. Scripture underlines the point that the knowledge of humanity pales in comparison to the knowledge of God. That human reasoning cannot begin to compare with divine reasoning is a point that the Book of Job makes. After some thirty-seven chapters of Job defending himself against God, and of Job's friends accusing him of unrighteousness, God himself finally enters onto the scene in a whirlwind with the words, "Who is this that darkens my counsel with words without knowledge?" (Job 38:2). For four chapters God then emphasizes his greatness—in part by noting the puniness of human wisdom. Job responds with contrition: "I have uttered what I did not understand, things too wonderful for me, which I did not know" (Job 42:4). Job learned that the truth of God is beyond human reasoning. A Psalmist also stressed this truth:

> When I look at your heavens, the work of your fingers, the moon and the stars that you have established; what are human beings that you are mindful of them, mortals that you care for them? (Ps 8:3–4)[1]

Speaking through Isaiah, the LORD could similarly say,

> For my thoughts are not your thoughts, nor are your ways my ways, says the LORD. For as the heavens are higher than the earth, so are my ways higher than your ways and my thoughts than your thoughts. (Isa 55:8–9)

The subject of human and divine reasoning finds a curious twist in the New Testament. To be sure, the finitude of human reasoning continues to be underscored—as with Paul's famous declaration: "For now we see in a mirror, dimly, but then we will see face to face. Now I know only in part; then I will know fully, even as I have been fully known" (1 Cor 13:12). But the concern is not so much that of contrasting divine and human reasoning. It is, rather, to show that the immensity of God's wisdom is, paradoxically, demonstrated through what humanity regards as base. God's wisdom is not mirrored in astounding human achievements or in philosophical ideas, but in what is homely, even loathsome—for God redeemed humanity not through political eloquence or might, but through the execution of a Jewish peasant. Paul contrasts human and divine wisdom in a letter to the Corinthians:

> Where is the one who is wise? Where is the scribe? Where is the debater of this age? Has not God made foolish the wisdom of the world? For since, in the wisdom of God, the world did not know God through wisdom, God decided, through the foolishness of our proclamation, to save those who believe. For Jews demand signs and Greeks desire wisdom, but we proclaim Christ crucified, a stumbling block to Jews and foolishness to Gentiles, but to those who are the called, both Jews and Greeks, Christ the power of God and the wisdom of God. For God's foolishness is wiser than human wisdom, and God's weakness is stronger than human strength. (1 Cor 1:20–25)

1. Throughout this work I will be using the *New International Version* (1984) of the Bible (the only exceptions being when I alter it to use inclusive language, or to highlight a particular word in the Hebrew or Greek).

Born Again and Beyond

The way in which God's wisdom is made manifest is altogether counterintuitive. Greeks looked for esoteric philosophy, and Jews demanded demonstrations of the miraculous. But the truth of God manifested itself through the crucifixion of Jesus—an idea that was reprehensible both to Jews and Greeks.

Through much of its history, the church has rightly taught that the truth of God far surpasses human wisdom, and such truth is mysterious. Declarations such as "God became incarnate in Jesus," "Jesus was wholly human and wholly divine at the same time," and "Jesus died for sinners" are altogether true—yet none of them can be fathomed. They are neither rational, nor irrational, but altogether supra-rational. Similarly, the doctrine of the Trinity cannot be understood rationally. The teaching that three interdependent divine persons commingle in the one God is true, but it exceeds human comprehension. Attempts to explain such mysteries are only fruitful insofar as they lead the worshipper to awe and devotion.

We need not apologize for the inability to conceptualize divine mysteries, for the contention that Christian faith is ultimately based on mystery is consistent with the very nature of spiritual existence. Every individual in the human race has what some have referred to as "God-consciousness." The author of Ecclesiastes stated that God "has put eternity into the hearts" of all people (Eccl 3:11). Paul similarly implied that a universal religious conscience exists (Rom 2:14–15). This holds true for the devout and the agnostic, for the believer and the atheist, for the religiously minded and the humanist, for the philanthropist and the hedonist—contrary to what they might say, all humanity is wired for belief in God. At some level, the truth of God therefore confronts the individual even prior to their thinking about it. This should not surprise us, for it is not as if people live without any awareness of God prior to being presented with the God question. Paul's address to the Athenian philosophers is here illustrative of this point. Rather than presenting the Athenians with a specific "plan of salvation," Paul started with the lowest common denominator that he shared with them:

> I see that in every way you are very religious. For as I walked around and looked carefully at your objects of worship, I even found an altar with this inscription: TO AN UNKNOWN GOD. Now what you worship as something unknown I am going to proclaim to you. (Acts 17:22–23)

St. Anselm's dictum is here on the mark: "I believe in order that I might understand." Embracing religious truth begins with belief; understanding follows belief. We may try to embrace religious truth by seeking to understand it first, and this may be somewhat profitable. But even here, there comes a point in time in which supra-rational decisions must be made to embrace God and be embraced by God. I think also of the famous dictum of Blaise Pascal: "the heart has its reasons of which reason knows nothing." Human rationality is entirely unable to probe all truth.

The relationship between the Bible and religious truth was brought home to me while I was the president of a Baptist seminary in rural Nigeria. I loved life there: whether it was teaching classes, piping spring water to the seminary compound, enhancing the morale of my community, or witnessing my wife Suzanne tending to the medical needs of people. I had many eureka moments in which I learned that my assumptions concerning the basic make-up of the world or of how things ought to be done were contrary to those assumptions that the community had. I can remember one of my students saying, "I'm sorry for falling asleep in your class today, but I haven't eaten for two days." That conversation proved to be a turning point in my understanding of why I was in Nigeria. Although the task assigned to me (from the head office in Chicago) was that of enhancing the level and quality of education at the seminary in Nigeria, I started to think that the basic needs of my students and their families, together with the basic needs of other instructors and their families, was not less important than educational matters. Students cannot concentrate on their studies when their children are suffering from malnourishment or disease, or when they themselves are hungry. Another eureka moment came to me during a course that I was teaching on Genesis. After the final lecture on the creation story, I asked my students, "How many of you believe that this story is essentially metaphoric and poetic, and how many of you believe that this story is essentially historic and scientific?" Much to my surprise, only a few students believed that Genesis 1–2 was essentially historic while the vast majority believed that these chapters were mostly metaphoric. Had I asked the same questions to typical Baptist seminarians anywhere in North America, the results would have been just the opposite. I was reminded of the fact that one's presuppositions concerning the nature of truth often determine the conclusions that are drawn. There is no question that my students in Nigeria believed that Genesis 1–2 was altogether true. Whether or not creation unfolded the way in which these chapters record is an entirely different matter. For such students, as was the case for that segment of Nigerian culture, truth was often conveyed through story. Rather than only giving yes or no answers, these Nigerians were at times inclined to recount stories—particularly so when shame was involved in some way. This is so unlike how "more advanced" folk think of truth as data that can be historically or scientifically investigated.

I find the notion that truth is principally conveyed through story to be most refreshing. Among other points, the truth of Genesis 1–2 has everything to do with its conception of the nature of God, the ideal nature of humanity, and the relation between the sexes. Conveying knowledge about the complexity of God or humanity is best done through stories. It is not as if Genesis could capture the subtle nuances of what it means to be human through a factual list of cold descriptions such as "people need each other" or "people want approval from others." A more engaging way of presenting this topic is to show through story what it means to be human. This, I believe, is equally true of understanding the nature of God. It would be painfully dull for Genesis to provide a list of the attributes of God—as if it was written for budding "theologians." More helpful than the bald statement "God is holy" is the story that has God casting the first couple from paradise because of their rebellion.

In the following paragraphs I will discuss two test cases, the first being Genesis 1, and the second being Matthew 1. I will contend that while such texts from the Bible are to be taken altogether seriously, understanding them in a literalistic manner does them great injustice.

Test Case #1: Genesis 1:1—2:4a

For those who take Genesis 1 literally, scientific and literary gymnastics need to be made in order to justify the text in light of scientific discoveries. Examples of such gymnastics include the "Gap Theory" and the "Age-Day Theory." According to the Gap Theory, dinosaurs (the existence of which poses a difficulty for a literal reading of Genesis 1) lived and died after verse one and before verse two. In this system of thought, "In the beginning God created the heavens and the earth" (v. 1) refers to a perfect creation. Immediately following this creation there was a great cataclysm in which the dinosaurs perished. This is suggested, or so it is maintained, with "Now the earth was formless and void and the spirit of God was hovering over the face of the deep" (v. 2): things had become less than perfect, so God was compelled to re-create the universe. In order to do some justice to the geological and fossil records, the Age-Day Theory similarly seeks to understand the six "days" as six "ages." Genesis 1 does not, according to this theory, refer to six twenty-four hour days, but six ages. Still others posit that the earth is only between six and ten thousand years old, rather than the more than four billion years that scientists posit.

It does not take a scholar to see that the "Gap Theory" is based on a highly suspect argument from silence. As for the "Age-Day Theory," it suffers from the fact that while the Hebrew word *yōm* ("day") does at times refer to a given age, it clearly refers to twenty-four hour days in Genesis 1—for throughout this chapter the days end with "there was evening and there was morning," an expression that denotes a twenty-four hour day. Note also that the justification given for Israel to keep the Sabbath day is that whereas the Lord made heaven and earth and all that is in them "in six days," he rested on "the seventh day" (Exod 20:11). With regard to the age of the earth, arguments in support of a young earth always start from a literal reading of Genesis 1 rather than scientific data itself.

Such theories do little more than foist a modern scientific worldview upon an ancient text, whose writer was not the least bit interested in such physically-bound matters. The given theories are, in fact, altogether worldly insofar as they start with the assumption that Genesis 1 can only be true if it is in accord with scientific data. Truth thus becomes the servant of science. But as I contended above, truth cannot be limited to that which can be historically or scientifically verified. Genesis 1 faithfully points to who God and humanity are, and the description of the creative acts on each successive day are recounted to furnish a correct understanding of the nature of God and humanity.

Prior to defending my contention that Genesis 1 is primarily concerned with providing an accurate understanding of who God is and who people are, it is important to say something about the religious mindset of people in the ancient Near East. Peoples in this world typically regarded themselves as being subject to the unpredictable and capricious actions of the gods: if the ground or a womb was thought to be infertile, if pestilence had come over the land, if the rains had not come, if a child died, if one became poor, or if the nation was conquered by another, it was because of the gods. Whatever came about did so because one or more of the gods was pleased or displeased for one reason or another, or perhaps because one god had been upstaged or defeated by another. It is to such a mindset that Genesis 1 originally spoke. Genesis 1 implicitly challenges this understanding of the nature of the divine world and humanity.

Born Again and Beyond

Differences between the Hebrew conception of God and humanity and ancient Near Eastern conceptions may be seen from a comparison between the *Enuma Elish* (the Babylonian creation story that concerns the pre-eminence of the god Marduk) and Genesis 1. In the *Enuma Elish*, Marduk takes his position as chief god of the Babylonian pantheon after killing various other gods. Demi-gods then complained to Marduk that they were tired of offering sacrifices to the gods that were above them. The demi-gods therefore pleaded with Marduk to make a species that would relieve them of this task. Marduk agreed with them and thereupon killed one of the gods who did not side with him earlier, and with this god's blood he made humanity—whose sole purpose for existence was to offer sacrifices to the superior gods. Unlike the creation of humanity in Genesis 1, then, humanity comes into existence in the *Enuma Elish* as an afterthought—whose sole function was to placate the gods with sacrifices. Contrary to the *Enuma Elish*, in the sixth day of Genesis 1 humanity is anything but an afterthought: humanity is the climax of the created order, the very image of God, and everything in creation exists for humanity.

That humanity is the pinnacle of creation in Genesis 1 is likewise evident from a comparison between it and other ancient literature. In the ancient world a king who commissioned a governor to rule on his behalf was said to be in the "image" of that king. It was expected that those who were subservient to the king would likewise be subservient to his governor, his "image." Various Egyptian texts recount how a pharaoh might be the "image" or "likeness" of one god or another. The eighth-century BC Pharaoh Piye could say of himself, "I am a king, divine emanation, living image of [the god] Atum" (from the stela of Piye), even as Thutmose IV could refer to himself as "living image of the All-Lord" (on the sphinx stela of Thutmose IV).[2] The image motif is particularly pronounced in the name-change of Tutankhaten ("living image of Aten") to Tutankhamen ("living image of Amen") in the twentieth century BC. Offspring and successors of the pharaohs were similarly thought to bear their "image." We see this, for example, in *The Teaching of King Amenemhet I to his son Senusret*: "O you living images of me, my heirs among men, make for me a funeral oration." Demi-gods of the Egyptian pantheon of gods were likewise regarded as being in the image of superior deities—a favorite of whom was the god Re.

---

2. All quotations of Egyptian literature are from *www.reshafim.org.il/ad/egypt/search.html*.

Genesis 1 challenges this common view. It is not only the pharaoh or king who is in the image of a god, for all humanity, "male and female" are in the image of God. Applying "image of God" language to all humanity made humanity significant. Because humanity shared God's image and likeness, it ruled creation. In this regard there is a striking parallel between what various Egyptian gods could say to different pharaohs and what God said of humanity. There are many examples in ancient Egyptian literature in which gods told pharaohs that the pharaohs were created in their image and that, as the representatives of the gods, they were to "rule" and have "dominion" over every aspect of the physical land. The parallels between such literature and later biblical literature are here unmistakeable—particularly with reference to the sixth day of creation:

> God created humankind in his image, in the image of God he created them; male and female he created them. God blessed them, and God said to them, "Be fruitful and multiply, and fill the earth and subdue it; and have dominion over the fish of the sea and over the birds of the air and over every living thing that moves upon the earth." (Gen 1:27–28)

According to both Egyptian literature and Genesis, then, the one who is in the image of the divine was also to rule over the earth. Genesis thus applies to all humanity the notion that the divine image was to rule over the earth, such was humanity's worth. Genesis thus democratizes "image of God" language—for it is not simply the king who bears the image of God, but all humanity is in God's likeness (and every individual is therefore of inestimable worth).

There are also features of Genesis 1 that similarly suggest that its author sought to provide a better understanding of the divine world. Genesis 1 includes elements of what may be referred to as a de-sacralization of the cosmos. When one looked into the sky and saw *šameš* (pronounced "sha-mesh") or the sun, one did not think of a ball of fire that was some 150 million kilometers away. Many in the ancient world believed that the sun was a deity, which they named *šamaš* (pronounced "sha-mash") and when one looked into the night sky and saw *yareach* (pronounced "ya-ray-akh") or the moon, one did not think of a physical body that orbited the earth, for many in the ancient world believed that the moon was a deity, who was named *yareach*. In Genesis 1 we read neither of the moon nor of the sun. We instead read of "the lesser light" and "the greater light" (vv. 14–16). By not referring to *yareach* or *šameš*, the author of Genesis 1 subtly made the point that the moon and the sun are, like the rest of creation, physical objects rather than deities.

One need not be acquainted with ancient Near-Eastern literature in order to determine what Genesis 1 concerns, for literary features of Genesis 1 also support the contention that this text is principally concerned with providing accurate understandings of the nature of God and of humanity. In contrast with the preceding days of creation—which receive three verses (days one and two), four verses (day five), or five verses (days three and four)—day six (on which humanity was created) receives eight verses. Humanity, moreover, was created "in the image and likeness of God" (vv. 26–27), it was to "rule over all the earth" (vss. 26, 28); and whereas on the previous five days the God said that what he created was "good" (vv. 4, 10, 12, 18, 21), following the creation of humanity God said that it was "very good" (v. 31).

The entire account of Gen 1:1—2:4a is itself structured in a masterful fashion. The ending of the unit (Gen 2:4a) mirrors the beginning of the unit (Gen 1:1) to create what is known as an inclusio.

Genesis 1:1	Genesis 2:4a
"In the beginning God created the heavens and the earth."	"In the day that the LORD God made the earth and the heavens."

Within this inclusio there is what is known as a chiasm—an A, B, B', A' literary structure: at the beginning of the account the order is "heavens and earth" (1:1) whereas at the end of the account the order is reversed to "earth and heavens" (2:4a).

In the table below, we see that the days of creation are themselves structured as panels in which days one, two and three (panel 1) are mirrored in days four, five, and six (panel 2). Prior to creation the earth was "formless and empty" (1:2). What we see in the six days of creation is God reversing this situation by filling formlessness with form. The first three days involve God separating things, and in the last three days things are created that were to inhabit and rule what was made in the first three days. Days one and four correspond to each other in terms of the creation of spheres and the filling of such spheres: on day one light is created, and on day four the inhabitants of such spheres are brought into existence—the sun, the moon, and the stars. Days two and five similarly correspond to each other: on day two the sea and the sky are created, and on day five that which inhabits the seas and the skies (fish and birds) are created. Days three

Truth and the Bible

and six correspond in the same way: land is created on day five, and on day six animals and humans are created. Gen 1:1—2:4a is thus arranged in the following way:

Panel One			*Panel Two*	
Day One:	light	⟷	Day Four:	sun, moon, stars
Day Two:	sky, sea	⟷	Day Five:	birds, fish
Day Three:	land	⟷	Day Six:	animals, humanity

Knowing the structure of Genesis 1 saves us from fanciful interpretations. Upon noting that according to Gen 1:3 light came into existence before the sun (Gen 1:14), rather creative interpretations have been given over the centuries. One interpretation is that the light spoken of in day one is a spiritual light whereas the light generated by the sun on the fourth day is a physical light. Another common interpretation is that whereas the light of 1:3 was scattered and confused, in 1:14 it was collected and henceforth proceeded from the luminaries. Such imaginative attempts to explain away the seeming tension between 1:3 and 1:14 are based on the assumption that Genesis 1 provides a sequential outline of the order of creation. But the concern is not the order of creation. The concern, rather, was to present God as thoughtful, not capricious, and creation as purposeful, not haphazard.

But the seventh day of the first week is particularly significant. Although humanity may be the climax of the six days of creation, it is the seventh day that is the pinnacle of the first week. To be sure, God created all things for humanity. But he created humanity for himself and the purpose of humanity is to enjoy perpetual rest in God (see Isa 45:18, "he did not create [the earth] a chaos, he formed it to be inhabited"). A close reading of Gen 2:2–3 in light of its context supports this interpretation. Among other points, the seventh day differs from the first six days insofar as it is only with the seventh day that there is no mention of "evening and morning." An ancient interpretation of this teaches that the seventh day has no ending. As such, it is perpetually open and the opportunity to enter into eternal rest with God is available for all—as the author of Hebrews makes clear:

> For somewhere he has spoken about the seventh day in these words: "And on the seventh day God rested from all his work."
> ... There remains, then, a Sabbath-rest for the people of God; for anyone who enters God's rest also rests from his own work, just as

God did from his. Let us, therefore, make every effort to enter that rest. (Heb 4:4, 9–11)

This interpretation of Genesis 1 may be looked down upon by some because it does not address the creation/evolution argument. But let us remember that a key feature of Biblical interpretation is to interpret Scripture in light of the ancient culture in which it was written. This is a common practice among biblical scholars, who are rightly wary of imposing modern or Western concerns upon the ancient Scriptures. Yet this is precisely what is done to Genesis 1 when the assertion is made that this text is fundamentally opposed to evolutionary theory. Genesis 1 did not have modern science or evolutionary theory in mind when it was written. This chapter was written millennia before such concerns in a very different world—a world that had little regard for humanity, a world enslaved by the gods. It was for such a world that Genesis 1 was written. A scientific worldview did not exist, nor, let it be said, did Charles Darwin's theory of evolution. Let us take Scripture seriously by asking what it meant even before we ask what it means. The worth of humanity before God was the central concern, and while evolutionary theory may be taken to task for threatening this concern, it is wrong-headed to suppose that Genesis 1 is about "the how" rather than "the who" of creation.

Test Case #2: Matthew 1

As with the beginning of the Old Testament, the beginning of the New Testament provides a fine example of how the authors of the Bible had very different concerns than many modern-day interpreters of the Bible.

In the ancient Hebrew world genealogies were rarely simply concerned with outlining someone's ancestral heritage. One function of genealogies in the Bible is to prepare the reader for the stories that followed by anticipating the nature or work of one or more of the characters. Another function of genealogies is to comment on the nature of a family line or era. The first genealogy of the Bible (in Genesis 4) thus informs the reader that the line of Cain was murderous, even bloodthirsty (the first person of the genealogy, Cain, was a murderer, as was Lamech, the last person in the genealogy). The second genealogy of the Bible (in Genesis 5) provides a contrast with the murderous line of Cain by telling the reader of the righteous line of Seth. It is in this genealogy that one reads of Enoch who did not die (Gen 5:24) as well as Methuselah, who famously lived for 969 years (Gen 5:27)—the very year that the flood commenced! While there are many more genealogies in the rest of the Old Testament, there are only two genealogies in the New Testament—both of which concern Jesus. An important feature of Luke's genealogy of Jesus is that it concludes by mentioning Adam, who was "the son of God" (Luke 3:38). Referring to Adam in the genealogy of Jesus provides a contrast between Adam and the "second man" (1 Cor 15:45–49), Jesus Christ. More to the point, as the first Adam was "the son of God" insofar as he was the first man, Jesus is declared to be "the Son of God" by virtue of his resurrection from the dead (Rom 1:4).

The other genealogy in the New Testament is found in Matthew 1. This genealogy goes from Abraham to Joseph the human father of Jesus. There are two striking features of this genealogy. The first is that while more than forty men are mentioned, only five women are mentioned. The four women have two things in common. They were all gentiles, and their offspring came as a result of sexually illicit activities: Tamar seduced her father-in-law Judah (Genesis 38); Rahab was a prostitute (Joshua 2); Bathsheba had extra-marital relations with David (2 Samuel 11); and Ruth had a curious pre-marital liaison with Boaz on the threshing floor during the night (Ruth 3). This is all in contrast to Mary the wife of Joseph, who was both a Jewess and a virgin. Matthew evidently drew this contrast to underscore the point that God uses the most unlikely candidates to further his kingdom—unchaste gentile women. Indeed, throughout his Gospel Matthew emphasizes the point that while God would bring to fruition the promises made to the Patriarchs through the Jewish people, he would nevertheless use non-Israelites, tax-collectors, prostitutes, and "sinners" to do so. The second striking feature of the genealogy in Matthew 1 concerns its preoccupation with numerology. Matthew concludes his genealogy by stating that "there were fourteen generations in all from Abraham to David, fourteen from David to the exile to Babylon, and fourteen from the exile to the Christ" (Matt 1:17). David here figures prominently because, for Matthew, Jesus was the long-awaited messiah or Davidic King. The number fourteen was important for Matthew because it was the numeric equivalent in Aramaic of the name David. Let me be more specific. Each letter in the twenty-two letter Aramaic alphabet had a corresponding numeric value, so *aleph* (א) the first letter in the alphabet was one, *beth* (ב) the second letter in the alphabet was two, *gimel* (ג) the third letter in the alphabet was three, *dalet* (ד) the fourth letter in the alphabet was four, *heh* (ה) the fifth letter in the alphabet was five, *waw* (ו) the sixth letter in the alphabet was six, and so on. In Aramaic (and Hebrew), David is spelled ד ו ד (*dalet, waw, dalet*), the numeric equivalence being four plus six plus four—which equals fourteen. The fact that the history of Israel from Abraham to Jesus could readily be divided into three sections of fourteen generations each made this ideal for Matthew. Matthew's understanding of the nature of history is certainly fascinating, but we must note that while Matthew lists fourteen generations from Abraham to David, and fourteen generations from David to the Babylonian exile, he only lists thirteen generations from the exile to Jesus—yet he nevertheless emphasizes that there were three sets of fourteen generations each (Matt 1:17). Matthew certainly knew this, so in order to make up for the missing generation, and to retain the important number fourteen, he was evidently compelled to list Jehoiachin twice—once at the end of the second grouping of fourteen generations, and once at the beginning of the third grouping. Fanciful and ingenious interpretations have been created to solve this "difficulty." But the difficulty is ours, not that of the biblical text. As is so often the case in the Bible, what we moderns regard as faithful recording of history was not what the ancients thought was important. More than events themselves, biblical authors were concerned with *the significance of such events* in the light of God's redemptive activity. We appreciate the biblical story most fully when we seek to determine the intentions of the biblical authors (and when we ask ourselves how such concerns might differ from our own).

I have limited the conversation to two test cases—Genesis 1 and Matthew 1. One could easily draw similar conclusions with most every other chapter of the Bible. My concern, however, is not to show how one or another chapter might be understood. I only appeal for humility in biblical interpretation. Let us all recognize that we are quick to impose our ideas upon the biblical text and slow to investigate the concerns of the biblical text itself. A very low view of Scripture is really one in which Scripture is squeezed and forced into a doctrinal mold (e.g., "biblical inerrancy"), whereas a high view of Scripture allows Scripture to speak for itself.

Chapter Two

The Authority of the Bible

THE MOST PIVOTAL TEACHING of Evangelicalism is its understanding of the nature of Scripture. In the Evangelical mind, everything stands or falls on this understanding. If this doctrine is toyed with, the whole system of thought is threatened. Why? Simply because the Bible is thought to be *the* vehicle through which God has communicated his truth. It follows (for Evangelicalism) that if the Bible is somehow less than perfect, then the gospel story itself also falls short of perfection.

To safeguard its view of the Bible, Evangelicalism has applied different adjectives to it. The Bible is said to be "infallible" and/or "inerrant." Different authors use these words in different ways. For some, the Scriptures are said to be infallible insofar as the message that they proclaim is in accord with God's will for humanity. Others, who purportedly have a higher view of Scripture, prefer to use the word *inerrant*: the original autographs of the Scriptures are thought to have been without any error whatsoever with respect to science, history, logic, inner consistency, psychology, and the like. While I wholeheartedly concur that the message of the Bible is infallible insofar as it contains "all things necessary for salvation," I have huge problems with the view that Scripture is anything close to being inerrant.

For years now I have asked various Evangelical pastors and leaders why they believe that the Bible is the inerrant word of God. Not on a single occasion has a satisfactory answer ever been provided. Here are various answers that have been given to me.

Born Again and Beyond

- *"The Bible is the word of God because it is inerrant."*

It is maintained that one can know that the Bible was inspired by God because it lacks errors: even though it was written on different continents over more than one thousand years by dozens of authors, the Bible perfectly recounts history, it is in accord with true science, and it never contradicts itself. One very real problem with this view is that almost all biblical scholars (who have spent their lives studying ancient manuscripts of the biblical text) would contend just the opposite: there are scores of inconsistencies and historical errors in the Bible. It is only those who tie their faith to an inerrant view of the Bible who feel obliged to defend the Bible at every level. Perhaps more significantly, a problem with this notion is that it makes divine authority the servant of inerrancy; but the Bible is authoritative because it is from God, not because it is inerrant.

- *"One cannot have certainty that the gospel is true if one does not at the same time believe in the inerrancy of Scripture."*

This common reason given in support of the doctrine of inerrancy is based on a slippery slope assumption: if, it is maintained, parts of the Bible are not inerrant, it follows that one cannot have ultimate trust in its overall message—particularly with regard to the story of Jesus. Years ago I remember a preacher saying with great gusto, "If you can't believe that the serpent at one time was with legs [i.e., because he was cursed to crawl on his belly], then you can't believe in anything in the Bible." This may well be an extreme example, but it does underline the absurdity of the slippery slope argument. Belief in the gospel is in no way tied to belief in the inerrancy of all of Scripture. One can legitimately believe that while the gospel story may not be historically perfect at every point, it nevertheless faithfully testifies to the truth of God in Christ.

- *"The Bible is the inerrant word of God because it declares itself to be such."*

A common passage used to support this assertion is the following.

> All Scripture is God-breathed and is useful for teaching, rebuking, correcting and training in righteousness, so that the man of God may be thoroughly equipped for every good work. (2 Tim 3:16–17)

A straightforward reading of this passage suggests that it has nothing to say about whether or not the Bible is inerrant. It only says that Scripture is "useful" for pastoral matters, such as "teaching, rebuking, correcting and training in righteousness." Not a word is said about inerrancy, its historical exactitude, its scientific truth, or even its inner consistency.

Here is another passage.

> Above all, you must understand that no prophecy of Scripture came about by the prophet's own interpretation, for prophecy never had its origin in the will of man, but men spoke from God as they were carried along by the Holy Spirit (2 Pet 1:20–21).

The concern of this passage is the nature of the prophetic word within Scripture—as, for example, in a prophetic book such as Isaiah or Hosea. Even if this passage refers to the entire Old Testament, it says nothing more than that Scripture was inspired by the Holy Spirit. Supposing that it refers to inerrancy is to impose one's ideology upon the text.

But even if such passages referred to the inerrancy of the Old Testament (the New Testament did not exist when 2 Timothy and 2 Peter were written), there would still be a very real problem with the assertion that "*The Bible is the inerrant word of God because it declares itself to be such.*" Such logic is clumsy, for it presupposes the very point that it wishes to prove. If we were consistent with such reasoning we would be led to conclude that the *Koran* and the *Book of Mormon* are also the word of God, for both works declare themselves to be such. The following is from the *Koran*.

> And if ye are in doubt as to what we have revealed from time to time to our servant, then produce a Sura like thereunto; and call your witnesses or helpers (if there are any) besides Allah, if your (doubts) are true *(002.023)*.

Here are two examples from the *Book of Mormon*.

> And when ye shall receive these things, I would exhort you that ye would ask God, the Eternal Father, in the name of Christ, if these things are not true; and if ye shall ask with a sincere heart, with real intent, having faith in Christ, he will manifest the truth of it unto you, by the power of the Holy Ghost. (Moroni 10:4)

> And God shall show unto you, that that which I have written is true. (Moroni 10:29)

Simply because the *Koran* and the *Book of Mormon* make the claim that they are true does not make them true.

- *"The Bible is the inerrant word of God because of the amazing storyline."*

It is noted that the Bible was written over many centuries by many different authors with many different concerns, yet because the Bible nevertheless maintains an amazing storyline, it must be the inerrant word of God. Once again, the conclusion does not follow the observations. Other religions make this claim about their Scriptures, but such a claim does not make their Scriptures true. One can take, for example, the centerpiece of Indian religious thought, the *Mahabharata*. This Scripture is many times the length of the Bible, and it, too, was written over many centuries by many different individuals with very different concerns; yet like the Bible, it nevertheless maintains an essential storyline. Maintaining a storyline over centuries speaks of the way in which a tradition has become integral to a community, which may not have anything to do with its God-given status.

- *"The Bible is the inerrant word of God because of the existence of prophecy and fulfillment."*

It is claimed that there are more than four hundred prophecies or predictions in the Old Testament concerning the coming Christ, and that all such predictions find their fulfillment in the story of Jesus. I have never seen a list of the four hundred (putative) prophecies; and even if one was produced I doubt very much that it would withstand even the kindest scrutiny. The common rebuttal, moreover, to the contention that predictive prophecy exists is that rather than Old Testament texts anticipating the New Testament story, New Testament authors based their writings upon Old Testament texts. But even if predictive prophecy exists (and I believe that it does), it does not follow that the entire Bible is the inerrant word of God.

- *"While the Bible of today may have errors in it, one can be confident that the original autographs were without error."*

This assertion is most problematic. First, because it is based on an argument from silence: because we do not possess original manuscripts, it is impossible to affirm or deny the assertion that the original manuscripts were without error. Second, the term "original" simply does not apply to the many books in the Bible that were edited over decades and even centuries before they became Scripture. Here are a few examples from the Pentateuch (Genesis–Deuteronomy). Throughout history, both Jewish and Christian tradition has attributed the whole of the Pentateuch to Moses. Yet things are not so simple as this. In two instances Genesis tells us that "the Canaanites were then in the land" (Gen 12:8; 13:8). The necessary

The Authority of the Bible

implication from this statement is that the Canaanites were no longer in the land—which situates us *after* the death of Moses. Again, Numbers tells us that "Moses was the humblest man on the face of the earth" (Num 12:3). If, indeed, Moses was a humble man, he could not have written this about himself! So also, the final passage of Deuteronomy concerns Moses's death and burial—which Moses certainly did not write but which was written at a later time. As with the other examples, it is here clear that this passage in Deuteronomy was added to the "original" text.

I now turn to the subject of the formation of the Bible. The Bible did not fall from heaven all at one time. Rather, not unlike a snowball that grows larger as it rolls down a hill, the Bible grew over the centuries as pieces of literature were added to it. The first section of the Bible to become Scripture was the Old Testament. Centuries later the New Testament was added. But one can easily break these up, for just as various sections of the Old Testament were added to it and became Scripture, so various sections of the New Testament were subsequently added to it and became part of Scripture. The way in which one or another piece of literature was written only to eventually become part of Scripture is known as the process of canonization. Using examples from the Old and New Testaments, in the paragraphs to follow I will briefly discuss how this process worked itself out.

The Pentateuch includes many features that suggest that it had a prehistory (i.e., the "author" relied on many earlier documents in the creation of the Pentateuch). Consider, for example, the following statements:

> This is the Book of Adam. When God created humanity, he made them in the likeness of God. (Gen 5:1)[1]

> That is why the Book of the Wars of the LORD says: ". . . Waheb in Suphah and the ravines, the Arnon and the slopes of the ravines that lead to the site of Ar and lie along the border of Moab." (Num 21:14–15)

In these two examples the author of the Pentateuch explicitly refers to books that recount the same information or, perhaps, from which he received his information.

One can only speculate about the contents of such books. It is reasonable to suppose that the "Book of Adam" included stories of Adam that

---

1. This is my own translation. The NIV of Genesis 5:1 is "this is the account of Adam's line." This translation, while not idiomatically inaccurate, fails to capture the literal wording of the Hebrew, which reads *sefer haadam*, "the book of Adam."

do not appear in Genesis. As for the "Book of the Wars of the LORD," perhaps its contents simply included a collection of the wars that the Israelites fought. If this is the case, then it might have been similar to the "Book of Jashar" that we read about in Joshua and 2 Samuel—for this book also evidently included information about various wars:

> So the sun stood still, and the moon stopped, till the nation avenged itself on its enemies, as it is written in the Book of Jashar. The sun stopped in the middle of the sky and delayed going down about a full day. (Josh 10:13)
>
> David . . . ordered that the men of Judah be taught this lament of the bow (it is written in the Book of Jashar). (2 Sam 1:18)

In addition to the fact that the author(s) of the Pentateuch explicitly referred to pre-existing *written* material upon which they may have depended, it is evident that they also relied on pre-existing material that was passed on *orally*. (Because relatively few people in the ancient world were literate, stories were typically passed on by word of mouth.) An example of this comes with *The Sargon Legend* and its parallels to the story of the birth of Moses in Exodus 2.

> My changeling mother conceived me, in secret she bore me. She set me in a basket of rushes, with bitumen she sealed my lid. She cast me into the river which rose over me. The river bore me up and carried me to Akki, the drawer of water. Akki, the drawer of water lifted me out as he dipped his ewer. Akki, the drawer of water, took me as his son and reared me.[2]
>
> Now a man of the house of Levi married a Levite woman, and she became pregnant and gave birth to a son. When she saw that he was a fine child, she hid him for three months. But when she could hide him no longer, she got a papyrus basket for him and coated it with tar and pitch. Then she placed the child in it and put it among the reeds along the bank of the Nile. His sister stood at a distance to see what would happen to him. Then Pharaoh's daughter went down to the Nile to bathe, and her attendants were walking along the river bank. She saw the basket among the reeds and sent her slave girl to get it. She opened it and saw the baby. He was crying, and she felt sorry for him. "This is one of the Hebrew babies," she

---

2. Ed. James R. Pritchard, *Ancient Near Eastern Texts Relating to the Old Testament*, 3rd ed. (Princeton: Princeton University Press, 1969), 119.

said. Then his sister asked Pharaoh's daughter, "Shall I go and get one of the Hebrew women to nurse the baby for you?" "Yes, go," she answered. And the girl went and got the baby's mother. Pharaoh's daughter said to her, "Take this baby and nurse him for me, and I will pay you." So the woman took the baby and nursed him. When the child grew older, she took him to Pharaoh's daughter and he became her son. She named him Moses, saying, "I drew him out of the water." (Exod 2:1–10)

The parallels between the stories of Moses and Sargon are clear: the birth of such leaders takes place in secrecy; baby Moses and baby Sargon are placed in reed baskets with caulking to float down a river; and both Moses and Sargon are then adopted by surrogates. Another parallel concerns the name Moses (which in Hebrew means "the one who draws [water]")—for in four instances the Sargon Legend refers to the "water drawer," while the Exodus story concludes with "She named him Moses, saying, 'I drew him out of the water.'" A pertinent question concerns dependence: was the Sargon Legend based on the story of Moses, was the story of Moses based on the Sargon Legend, or were both stories based on a common tradition? Answering this question involves knowing something about the dates of Sargon, Moses, and the literature pertaining to them—for if the Sargon Legend is much earlier than the story of Moses perhaps it is best to conclude that the story of Moses was based on the Sargon Legend. Sargon led the Akkadian dynasty in the late twenty-third and early twenty-second centuries BC, but the text of the Sargon Legend itself is only from the eighth century BC. With reference to Moses, he may have lived somewhere between the fifteenth and thirteenth centuries, but there is no consensus as to when Exodus was written—some suggest that it was written by Moses himself while others would contend that it (or much of it) was written somewhere between the tenth and eighth centuries BC. Proposed dates of Sargon and Moses, then, are of little help. In any case, it may well be that the two stories were based on a common tradition. The principal reason for holding this view is that elements of the Sargon and Moses accounts are found in stories of other political and religious leaders before the late second millennium BC and after the late first millennium BC.

There are many other stories in the Pentateuch that are very similar to ancient stories from the nations that surrounded Israel (stories about creation, about first humanity, about the gods, about kings, etc.). In addition to sharing stories, Israel's poetry, laws, and proverbs were all alike influenced to some degree by the literature of the surrounding nations. This is abundantly clear to anyone who has read such literature from the ancient world. Given the fact that even at its heyday under Solomon, Israel was but a tiny and seemingly insignificant nation, it is doubtful that the accounts of the surrounding nations were regularly based on Israel's accounts. While this may have been the case in a few instances, it certainly was not the case for the majority of instances. No doubt, Israel challenged the assumptions that underlay the literature of the surrounding nations, and without a doubt Israel modified most of what it borrowed; but borrow it certainly did.

The preceding paragraphs thus indicate that the composition of the Pentateuch took place over an extended period of time. What is true of the Pentateuch is equally true of most of the rest of the Bible. No, "original" books from the Bible did not float down from heaven into the minds of its divinely inspired authors. I am not in any way here challenging the belief that God inspired the writings of the Bible. I am only suggesting that many such writings had an involved pre-history.

I turn now to the subject of how various pieces of literature became Scripture. The doctrine of inerrancy is hard to accord with what we know about the formation of Scripture, for it is clear that tradition brought Scripture into existence. Yet this is precisely the opposite of what Evangelicalism teaches. Evangelicalism teaches that the early church created traditions on the basis of Scripture. But in the early decades of the Christian community the opposite was also true—for various traditions became Scripture as the believing community gave such traditions authority.

To begin with, there is no reason whatever to suppose that when the authors of New Testament letters thought that they were writing sacred Scripture. The rather incidental features of the letters suggest as much. If the author of 2 Timothy thought that he was writing Scripture, I doubt very much that he would have written "when you come, bring the cloak that I left with Carpus at Troas, and my scrolls, especially the parchments" (2 Tim 4:13). Similarly, if Paul thought that he was writing Scripture, he would not have written to the Galatians "see what large letters I use as I write to you with my own hand!" (Gal 6:11). If Paul thought that he was writing sacred Scripture I doubt very much that he would tell his Corinthian readers that he forgot whom he baptized:

> I thank God that I did not baptize any of you except Crispus and Gaius, so no one can say that you were baptized in my name. (Yes, I also baptized the household of Stephanas; beyond that, I don't remember if I baptized anyone else.) (1 Cor 1:14–16)

Nor would Paul have been so given to single out individuals if he thought that what he was writing would become sacred Scripture for all time: "I plead with Euodia and I plead with Syntyche to agree with each other in the Lord" (Phil 4:2); "some from Chloe's household have informed me that there are quarrels among you" (1 Cor 1:11). Indeed, most every letter of Paul closes with a list of individuals that are to be greeted, as with Romans 16:

> I commend to you our sister Phoebe, a servant of the church in Cenchrea. I ask you to receive her in the Lord in a way worthy of the saints and to give her any help she may need from you, for she has been a great help to many people, including me. Greet Priscilla and Aquila, my fellow workers in Christ Jesus. They risked their lives for me. Not only I but all the churches of the Gentiles are grateful to them. Greet also the church that meets at their house. Greet my dear friend Epenetus, who was the first convert to Christ in the province of Asia. Greet Mary, who worked very hard for you. Greet Andronicus and Junias, my relatives who have been in prison with me. They are outstanding among the apostles, and they were in Christ before I was. Greet Ampliatus, whom I love in the Lord. Greet Urbanus, our fellow worker in Christ, and my dear friend Stachys. Greet Apelles, tested and approved in Christ. Greet those who belong to the household of Aristobulus. Greet Herodion, my relative. Greet those in the household of Narcissus who are in the Lord. Greet Tryphena and Tryphosa, those women who work hard in the Lord. Greet my dear friend Persis, another woman who has worked very hard in the Lord. Greet Rufus, chosen in the Lord, and his mother, who has been a mother to me, too. Greet Asyncritus, Phlegon, Hermes, Patrobas, Hermas and the brothers with them. Greet Philologus, Julia, Nereus and his sister, and Olympas and all the saints with them.... Timothy, my fellow worker, sends his greetings to you, as do Lucius, Jason and Sosipater, my relatives. I, Tertius, who wrote down this letter, greet you in the Lord. Gaius, whose hospitality I and the whole church here enjoy, sends you his greetings. Erastus, who is the city's director of public works, and our brother Quartus send you their greetings.

Referring to all such individuals—whether they be relatives, apostles, leaders, converts, or "the city's director of public works"—suggests that Paul did not think that he was writing sacred Scripture to people some two thousand years later.

It is evident that Paul inherited teachings, and that he incorporated such teachings in his letters, and that years later the church community concluded that such letters should be regarded as Scripture. An example of this very natural process may be seen in 1 Corinthians 15:3–8:

> For what I received I passed on to you as of first importance: that Christ died for our sins according to the Scriptures, that he was buried, that he was raised on the third day according to the Scriptures, and that he appeared to Peter, and then to the Twelve. After that, he appeared to more than five hundred of the brothers at the same time, most of whom are still living, though some have fallen asleep. Then he appeared to James, then to all the apostles, and last of all he appeared to me also, as to one abnormally born.

Important for our purposes is Paul's statements that he "received" the teaching about the resurrection of Jesus and that he "passed on" such teaching to the Corinthians. In the early years of the church, the teaching about Jesus was passed down orally from one individual to another, and from one community to another. This was evidently before such a tradition was passed on in writing (most of the people were likely illiterate).

The contention that it was tradition that shaped Scripture in the first decades of the Christian community is also suggested from use of various sayings.

> Here is a trustworthy saying that deserves full acceptance: "Christ Jesus came into the world to save sinners." (1 Tim 1:15)

> Here is a trustworthy saying: "If anyone sets his heart on being an overseer, he desires a noble task." (1 Tim 3:1)

> Here is a trustworthy saying: "If we died with him, we will also live with him; if we endure, we will also reign with him. If we disown him, he will also disown us; if we are faithless, he will remain faithful, for he cannot disown himself." (2 Tim 2:11–13)

Such sayings (and many others besides) were cherished by the community of faith, and together with other traditions that were passed on orally, such sayings formed the basis of later Scriptural writings.

With reference to Paul's writings, the evolution from an individual letter to its becoming Scripture went something like the following. First, Paul wrote a letter to a specific community that addressed various issues that the community faced. Second, communities often shared such letters with one another:

> After this letter has been read to you, see that it is also read in the church of the Laodiceans and that you in turn read the letter from Laodicea. (Col 4:16)

Third, individual letters of Paul presumably circulated together as a collection. This may be seen in the fact that the letters that have traditionally been attributed to Paul were arranged from longest to shortest: Romans (16 chapters), 1 Corinthians (16 chapters), 2 Corinthians (13 chapters), Galatians (six chapters), Ephesians (six chapters), Philippians (four chapters), Colossians (four chapters), 1 Thessalonians (five chapters), 2 Thessalonians (three chapters), Philemon (one chapter). (The pastoral letters—1 Timothy, 2 Timothy, and Titus—were added to the collection later.) Similar to this process is the collection of the seven letters in Revelation 2–3. While such letters may have never circulated independently of one another, the fact that in Revelation 2–3 they are together suggests that it was common for groups of letters to be circulated together. The fourth and final stage of the process concerns the time in which Paul's letters were eventually regarded as Scripture. Not later than the early second century, the author of 2 Peter could refer to Paul's letters as Scripture:

> He writes the same way in all his letters, speaking in them of these matters. His letters contain some things that are hard to understand, which ignorant and unstable people distort, as they do *the other Scriptures*, to their own destruction. (2 Pet 3:16)

It is similarly difficult to accord the doctrine of inerrancy with the canonization of Scripture. ("Canonization" refers to the process in which the early church came to an [unofficial] conclusion regarding which books of the New Testament were Scripture.)

While this is an involved subject, the central features of the process of canonization of the New Testament are the following: in the mid-first century various letters from Paul were written; that at about this time some of the general epistles may have been written; that using very early oral traditions, the Gospels were written closer to the end of the first century; and that various other epistles and Revelation were written at the end of the first or beginning of the second century.

While it may not have been until the Council of Nicaea in AD 325 that the Church *officially* canonized the Old and New Testaments as we have them today, the church had *unofficially* regarded them as canon already in the second century, and the sacred traditions were regarded as being religiously authoritative already in the early first century. Various statements from the Church Fathers as well as the Muratorian canon (possibly late second century) indicate that in the second century the church had an unofficial canon. No doubt, several books from the New Testament were questioned as to their suitability. It took decades for such books as the Gospel of John, Hebrews, and Revelation to become canonical, while other books, such as the Shepherd of Hermas, were set aside.

Outside of second-century evidence from the Church Fathers and early church historians, there are various indications from the New Testament itself that the process of canonization took place over an extended period of time, and that books from the first century that were regarded as being religiously authoritative were evidently set aside in the second century as being unworthy of canonization. The epistle of Jude furnishes us with some examples, for in this short epistle there are three references to literature that was evidently at one time regarded as Scripture. In Jude 6 and 14–15 references are made to *The Book of Enoch*:

> And the angels who did not keep their positions of authority but abandoned their own home—these he has kept in darkness, bound with everlasting chains for judgment on the great Day.

> Enoch, the seventh from Adam, prophesied about these men: "See, the Lord is coming with thousands upon thousands of his holy ones to judge everyone, and to convict all the ungodly of all the ungodly acts they have done in the ungodly way, and of all the harsh words ungodly sinners have spoken against him."

So also, in Jude 9 reference is made to *The Assumption of Moses*:

> But even the archangel Michael, when he was disputing with the devil about the body of Moses, did not dare to bring a slanderous accusation against him, but said, "The Lord rebuke you!"

Jude's use of sacred literature that did not find its way into our canon of Scripture thus suggests that in his time the canon of Scripture had not been fixed.

It seems to me that, for many, simple trust in God is not enough. What is needed is a written text that unambiguously tells believers how to believe, think, and live. The desire for such a text is universal. Irrespective of where

The Authority of the Bible

we are in the world, seekers after spiritual truth feel compelled to legitimate and defend their faith on the basis of one Scriptural text or another. Do not get me wrong. I have no problem at all with religious texts. My concern is that believers all too often love the Scriptures and the doctrines surrounding them more than they love God or people, for it is easier to have a relationship with literature, which we can control through various means of interpretation, than it is to have a relationship with the living God, whom we cannot control in the least. In order to defend their faith before others or in their own minds, believers often come up with all sorts of unreasonable, even idolatrous arguments to support their understanding of the nature and function of their Scriptures.

In the Evangelical world, the word inerrant receives qualification upon qualification all in order to place the holy text on a certain and unshakeable foundation. A standard discussion goes something like this.

> "Is the Bible entirely consistent with science?" "Certainly it is. But (*qualification number one*), we must understand that the authors wrote of phenomena as they witnessed them. So, when the text says that the sun rose, whereas modern day people understand this metaphorically, ancient people literally believed that the sun rose. Moreover (*qualification number two*), where the Bible and science disagree, we must believe that the two will nevertheless be reconciled (either as a result of more thorough scientific investigation, or as a result of a better understanding of the Biblical text in question). Again (*qualification number three*), even where science and the Bible can never be reconciled, we must hold that the original manuscripts (*which do not exist*) nevertheless did not contradict science."

Rather than simply saying that the Bible is not inerrant, qualification follows upon qualification which follows upon qualification—"death by a thousand qualifications." Scores of books and articles are written, lectures are given, and sermons are preached—all to defend the doctrine of inerrancy. Dozens of books and booklets with such pretentious titles as the *Encyclopedia of Biblical Difficulties* are published, yet the Evangelical community is slow to say, "Maybe it's not the Bible that has difficulties. Maybe it's the things that we demand of the Bible in order to support our faith that create difficulties."

I am here reminded of the children's classic *The Emperor Has No Clothes*. No one along the road was willing to contradict the tailors of the king who said that the emperor's clothes were absolutely stunning in every way; and no one along the road was willing to embarrass the emperor—who himself thought that his finery must be of the grandest order because everyone seemed to be admiring it. It was an innocent little boy who first stated the obvious fact: the emperor was not wearing fine clothes; the emperor was, in fact, parading about in his underwear. So it is with the doctrine of inerrancy. The Evangelical community has unwittingly paraded its understanding of the Bible at the front and center for all to see. Yet such an understanding has no basis whatsoever. As the years pass, the world (rightly) laughs.

In a sadly ironic fashion, the Evangelical teaching that the Scriptures are inerrant is a most worldly way of looking at things. The notion that the Scriptures are divinely authoritative because they are inerrant situates divine authority below inerrancy. As I stated above, beginning in the eighteenth century, Evangelicalism (and with it, much of Christendom) rather unwittingly bought into Enlightenment mentality—a mentality that placed rationality, logic, and certitude above other ways of thinking. Truth cannot be known, so the Enlightenment project maintained, through religious teaching but only through human reasoning. In order to defend the authority of Scripture, Evangelicalism similarly contended that through reasoning one can see that the Scriptures are inerrant. The assumptions concerning truth that Evangelicalism adopted from the world told Evangelicalism how to understand its Scriptures, and every subsequent attempt to defend the doctrine of inerrancy has been based on such assumptions. This is what I mean by the statement that "the Evangelical teaching that the Scriptures are inerrant is a most worldly way of looking at things." Relegating truth to scientific precision or historical accuracy is not only naïve, but it is worldly in the extreme. Those who have life in God encounter truth at every turn. Yes, truth shows itself in history and science, but it equally does so in realms of beauty and ethics, religion and life-giving relationships, creation and even what is mundane. All existence cries out, "Look closely, not just with your eyes and mind, but also with your heart and spirit, and you will see glimpses of truth everywhere." Jesus could similarly declare, "Do you have eyes but fail to see, and ears but fail to hear?" (Mark 8:18).

It is simply not necessary for something to be inerrant before it can be authoritative. When we say, "The coach spoke with authority," the degree to which the coach's speech was inerrant is of little concern. The teammates concur that the speech was authoritative because it was marked by conviction and experience, because it brought the teammates out of their slump, or because the speech resonated with their understanding of their ability to win. So also, governing bodies and committees throughout the democratic world base their decision-making processes on *Robert's Rules of Order*. Authority is granted to this work primarily for pragmatic reasons: within a democratic body, it works. While *Robert's Rules of Order* is fully authoritative, such authority has nothing whatever to do with any inerrant qualities. Canon laws of various ecclesial bodies are also authoritative, yet their authority is based not on any inerrant qualities but on the will of the people who have chosen to function within such bodies.

It must be granted, then, that what is authoritative is not necessarily also inerrant. But can the same be said about the Bible, which the Christian community has traditionally thought of as having its authority in God? That is to say, because the Bible (unlike *Robert's Rules*) finds its authority in God, does it not follow that, like God, it must somehow be without error? No, there is simply no reason to conclude that the one follows from the other. The only perfect revelation of God is Jesus, who alone embodies the truth of God. Jesus, not Scripture, is referred to as "the wisdom of God" (1 Cor 1:25). Jesus, not Scripture, is "the Word" of God (John 1:1, 14). Jesus, not Scripture, radiates the glory of God (Heb 1:3). The only perfect revelation of God is the Son of God. Other forms of divine revelation, as powerful and compelling as they might be, can only pale in comparison to Jesus, in whom "the fullness of the Deity lives in bodily form" (Col 2:9). This is not to denigrate Scripture in any way. Scripture has the life-giving function of defining and shaping faith. Scripture faithfully recounts the Christ story. Scripture unfolds for believers the many promises of God. Scripture retains all that is necessary for salvation. As such, Scripture has a central role to play in the life of the church.

Up until this point I have been most critical of the Evangelical understanding of the nature of Scripture. You might then rightly ask, "How do you understand the nature of Scripture in the life of the believing community?" I will now present my view. Do note that I here say "my view." I am not remotely saying my view is the only correct view. Nor am I suggesting that thoughtful or committed Christians must make my view their own. The Bible is a God-given tool that points us to relationship with God. It is not the job of the church to tell the Spirit of God that he really ought to work in the believer's heart only through one particular understanding of the nature of the Bible. Yes, there are general parameters that should guide the reader—such as understanding Scripture in its historical and theological contexts, or interpreting Scripture through the lens of the Christ story.

But foisting a very specific model of understanding upon fellow Christians and saying that this model is the *only* model is, at best, unhelpful. At worst it is destructive to faith.

My interest in the Bible is largely pragmatic. The concern of the early church was that of preaching Christ crucified. Such preaching never concerned arguing about the historical or scientific veracity of Scripture. I will only defend what the Bible is, or refute what it is not, if doing so will make the way clear for preaching Christ crucified. My complaint about the doctrine of inerrancy is that it in fact obscures the gospel by asserting that a particular view of the Bible is fundamental to the gospel itself.

I begin with my understanding of the storyline of the Bible. I believe that the Bible is a great chiasm in which the latter part of the story is a mirror image of the first part of the story. Authors of Old Testament books often used a chiastic literary device to accentuate their message. A chiasm could be only one verse in length, a chapter, a section, or a complete book. A chiasm of only one verse may be seen in Gen 9:7.

    A   Whoever sheds
      B   the blood
        C   of man
        C'   by man
      B'   shall his blood
    A'   be shed

We see in this verse that close to the same thing is said twice, once forwards and once backwards. The author may have done this for lyrical reasons, for mnemonic reasons (i.e., to aid in memorization), or perhaps for stylistic reasons (i.e., the statement in Gen 9:7 has a fullness that it would not have otherwise).

A complete story that was pieced together chiastically is the story of the Tower of Babel (Gen 11:1-9).

The Authority of the Bible

```
A      all the earth had one language
    B      they said to each other
        C      come let us make ("laban") bricks
            D      let us build for ourselves
                E      a city and a tower
                    X      the LORD came down to see
                E'     the city and the tower
            D'     that the men were building
        C'     come let us confuse ("nabal")
    B'     they will not understand each other
A'     the language of all the earth
```

As with Gen 9:7, the second part of the story shares linguistic links with the first part of the story. Different from Gen 9:7 is that fact that this chiasm has a central point, X. The author's purpose in creating this chiasm was ironic. In terms of the central point, "The LORD came down to see," the author implicitly made the point that while the builders sought to make a tower that reached to the heavens, the LORD nevertheless had to come down from heaven to see what they were doing. Some tower! With regard to the corresponding sections, the irony is present insofar as whereas in the first section the people sought to make a name for themselves through particular actions, in the second section the LORD inverts their very actions. The irony here is altogether delightful in C and C': as the people said "come, let us make (Hebrew: *laban*) bricks," so the LORD said, "come, let us confuse (Hebrew: *nabal*)." The LORD thus inverted the very terminology that the people used (*nabal* is *laban* spelled backwards).

I think that the whole story in the Bible is itself an extended chiasm.

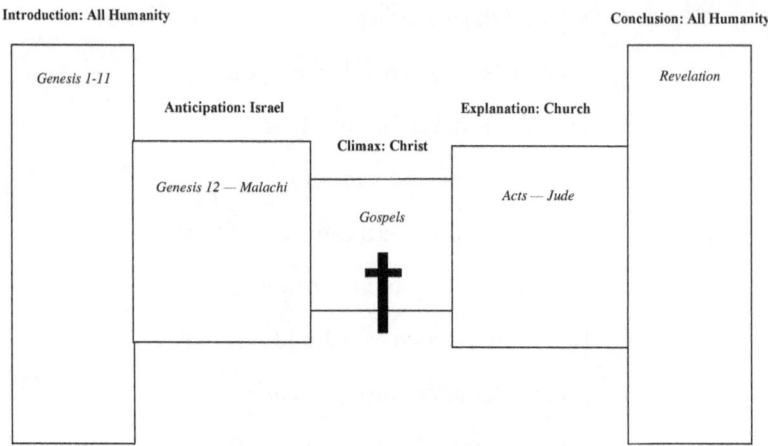

The introduction and the conclusion of the Bible mirror each other insofar as each concerns all humanity, perfect harmony with God, and the propensity toward evil that thwarts such harmony. Thematic and linguistic links that tie the beginning of Genesis to the end of Revelation include the following: whereas we read of "the curse" in early Genesis (e.g., Gen 3:17), so at the end of Revelation we read that "there will no longer be a curse" (Rev 22:3); whereas in early Genesis we read of "the tree of life" (Gen 2:9; 3:22, 24), so at the end of Revelation we read that "the tree of life is for the healing of the nations" (Rev 22:2); and whereas in early Genesis we find that God dwells close to humanity—breathing life into Adam, forming Eve, and living with them in the Garden—so at the end of Revelation we read that "the dwelling of God is with people, and he will live with them" (Rev 21:3). The ideal of paradise that we read about in Genesis 2 weaves its way through Scripture, and Scripture informs us that it is God's will to bring humanity back to this ideal. German theologians have rightly said, "Urzeit gleich Endzeit"—the beginning of time is like the end of time. Most of Genesis 12 to Jude is ultimately about bringing humanity back to paradise. The corresponding sections, Genesis 12–Malachi and Acts–Jude, concern this matter: whereas the twelve tribes of Israel came into existence in order to bring humanity back to God but failed to do so, the twelve disciples and the church came into existence to bring humanity back to God and they will (in spite of themselves!) succeed in doing so. More specifically, whereas Genesis 12–Malachi "anticipate" the coming of Christ and his kingdom, Acts–Jude "explain" or comment upon the coming of Christ and his kingdom. The climax of the story of the Bible is the gospel story. Jesus's teachings concerning the kingdom of God and his unsurpassed ethic bring to mind God's ideal in which harmony between God and humanity abounds. The pinnacle of this climax is the crucifixion and resurrection of Jesus, which will eventually restore humanity to that ideal state that we read of in the beginning of Genesis and the end of Revelation. It follows from this understanding of the Bible as an extended chiasm that pride of place is given to the beginning, center, and end of the Bible. The bulk of the Old Testament (Genesis 12–Malachi) and the bulk of the New Testament (Acts–Jude) fall outside this. (While I readily admit that my understanding of the movement of the story of the Bible along chiastic lines might be somewhat imaginative, I nevertheless think that seeing the overall story of the Bible along such lines can be most helpful.)

Without trying to sound overly self-confident, I suggest that Jesus's understanding of Scriptural revelation (which for him, only involved the Old Testament) is not unlike the foregoing discussion of the chiastic arrangement of Scripture—insofar as Jesus looked forward to the re-emergence of Eden in the kingdom of God. Before I become more specific, I want us to reflect on some passages in which Jesus's understanding of the Old Testament comes to the fore.

There are, to begin with, the so-called antitheses of Jesus in the Sermon on the Mount in Matthew 5. In each of the six antitheses of Jesus, Jesus quoted Moses only to challenge him. Here are the antitheses:

> You have heard that it was said to the people long ago, "Do not murder, and anyone who murders will be subject to judgment." But I tell you that anyone who is angry with his brother will be subject to judgment.

> You have heard that it was said, "Do not commit adultery." But I tell you that anyone who looks at a woman lustfully has already committed adultery with her in his heart.

> It has been said, "Anyone who divorces his wife must give her a certificate of divorce." But I tell you that anyone who divorces his wife, except for marital unfaithfulness, causes her to become an adulteress, and anyone who marries the divorced woman commits adultery.

Born Again and Beyond

> Again, you have heard that it was said to the people long ago, "Do not break your oath, but keep the oaths you have made to the Lord." But I tell you, do not swear at all: either by heaven, for it is God's throne; or by the earth, for it is his footstool; or by Jerusalem, for it is the city of the Great King.
>
> You have heard that it was said, "Eye for eye, and tooth for tooth." But I tell you, do not resist an evil person. If someone strikes you on the right cheek, turn to him the other also.
>
> You have heard that it was said, "Love your neighbor and hate your enemy." But I tell you: Love your enemies and pray for those who persecute you, that you may be sons of your Father in heaven."

Consistent with a traditional interpretation of the antitheses, it seems that Jesus was here taking Moses's teaching further. This interpretation is consistent with Jesus's use of Mosaic texts elsewhere. Consider, for example, Jesus's teaching about divorce in Matthew 19.

> Some Pharisees came to him to test him. They asked, "Is it lawful for a man to divorce his wife for any and every reason?" "Haven't you read," he replied, "that at the beginning the Creator 'made them male and female,' and said, 'For this reason a man will leave his father and mother and be united to his wife, and the two will become one flesh'? So they are no longer two, but one. Therefore what God has joined together, let man not separate." "Why then," they asked, "did Moses command that a man give his wife a certificate of divorce and send her away?" Jesus replied, "Moses permitted you to divorce your wives because your hearts were hard. But it was not this way from the beginning."

Some Pharisees tested Jesus—presumably to show that his understanding of the Mosaic law was fraudulent. They did so by quoting a passage from Deuteronomy that concerns divorce. As in other instances, Jesus's response suggests that Moses's law was simply in place because of the hardness and stubbornness of humanity: "Moses permitted you to divorce your wives because your hearts were hard." Jesus's conclusion that "it was not this way from the beginning," as well as his quotations of the Adam and Eve story, show that for him the ideal ethic is found in the Garden, and Moses's ethic was only put in place because of the sinfulness of humanity—it simply is not God's ideal.

The Authority of the Bible

Back, then, to my understanding of the Bible as an extended chiasm. Consistent with Jesus's view that Moses's law was interim because of the sinfulness of humanity, it is problematic for Christians of any stripe to insist that all of Scripture is on the same footing. The fact is that Scripture implodes upon itself. Scripture is, in a sense, self-destructing insofar as Jesus taught that Scripture's sole purpose is to point beyond itself to God. In this regard, Jesus said the following to the Pharisees:

> And the Father who sent me has himself testified concerning me. You have never heard his voice nor seen his form, nor does his word dwell in you, for you do not believe the one he sent. You diligently study the Scriptures because you think that by them you possess eternal life. These are the scriptures that testify about me, yet you refuse to come to me to have life. (John 5:37–40)

Sadly ironic is the fact that while the Pharisees "diligently" studied the Scriptures, God's "word" did not dwell in them. They were unable to see that the Scriptures pointed beyond themselves to Jesus. Scripture is not an end in itself, only a means to a greater end—faith in the supreme revelation of God, who alone is the inerrant Word of God, Jesus Christ. Whereas I happily agree that "all Scripture is God-breathed," this is not at all to say that all of it is equal—the beginning, the center, and the end together point to God's ideal.

In terms of historicity, I think that the Bible is hit and miss. More important than determining the degree to which biblical stories are historically accurate is learning how to read them in the first place. Biblical narrative is replete with signposts that tell the reader how to interpret things. Such signposts say things like, "here is irony," "here is satire," "here is characterization," "here is a lesson," or "here is history" (as, for instance, with the Exodus and the Christ stories). We do the Bible and its message grave injustice when we fail to read it carefully, or when we naively assume that it is only true insofar as it is historically true.

In terms of the Bible's consistency, a straightforward reading of it suggests that it contains a host of irreconcilable features. "Why," early readers of the Pentateuch might have asked, "do the ten commandments in Exodus 20 differ from the ten commandments in Deuteronomy 5?" "Why," the mediaeval rabbis asked, "did the Patriarchs do things that the law of Moses forbade?" "Why," they asked, "does Ezekiel prescribe sacrifices that are contrary to the laws of Moses?" "Why," Jean Astruc asked, "is the account of creation in Genesis 1 so different from that of Genesis 2?" "Why," the second-century Ebionites asked, "do the baptismal stories of Jesus in the Gospels differ from one another?" "Why," modern readers might ask, "does Jesus cleanse the temple at the end of his ministry in Matthew, Mark, and Luke, but he does so already at the beginning of his ministry in John?" One could quite easily write books about these and thousands of other discrepancies in the Bible. (Indeed, it has been done many times!) Especially with regard to ethics, there is a huge development. The Bible takes us from burning the sexually illicit and stoning blasphemers to forgiving wrongdoers. The Bible goes from the divine smiting of heathen (entire nations and "everything that breathes" within them) to divine love of the whole world. The Bible takes us from eye for eye mentality to turning the other cheek and blessing those who hurt us. Not unlike the imprecatory Psalms where the Psalmist pleads with God to injure in horrific ways one enemy or another, the Psalmist could even say that one who grabs a baby Babylonian by the heels and smashes its head against a rock is blessed (Ps 137:8–9). The difference between this and Jesus's teaching shouts to us: "Let the little children come to me, and do not hinder them, for the kingdom of heaven belongs to such as these" (Matt 19:14). No doubt, many theories regarding how to interpret such differences abound. Personally, I do not try to justify or explain away such differences. All such differences are, in my mind, products of the evolution of religious thinking, in which biblical authors readily equated their thoughts with the very will of God. I understand that this view might be off-putting to those who are more conservatively minded, but looking at things in this way is consistent with the over-arching story of the Bible—a story that goes from God's ideal, to the breakdown of that ideal, to the restoration of that ideal. As individuals evolve in their religious understanding, and as communities of faith do so as well, so there is movement within the story of the Bible itself.

My rather negative conclusion is that the whole Evangelical enterprise is based on a very shaky foundation—not Scripture or even the message of Scripture, but a dangerously naïve view of the nature and function of Scripture. No, Scripture is not inerrant. The contention that it is, is little more than the imposition of Enlightenment mentality on the life of faith. No, Scripture does not pretend to be inerrant. No verse in the Bible suggests as much. No, the original manuscripts were not inerrant. Such things do not exist, and in many instances they never did. No, Scripture did not precede tradition. The traditions, values, and beliefs of the early church community created Scripture. No, Scripture is not all equal. Scripture bows before God with all creation, and it freely confesses that it is but an instrument to point people to Jesus Christ and his kingdom. In my mind, viewing Scripture as the ultimate revelation is dangerously close to idolatry.

Chapter Three

Knowing and Doctrine

It is a commonplace to try to understand ways of living in terms of how such ways concern knowing, doing, or being—or some amalgamation thereof. Individuals likewise make decisions with respect to which member they favor in this knowing-doing-being triad—even if only at a subconscious level. For some, the predominant member of the triad is knowing. The concern here is with the ability to process and organize cognitive data, to understand not only the nature of various ideas, but to see how such ideas might interrelate with one another. Others favor doing. It is action that is important, not simply thinking about action. (I am here reminded of the famous statement of Karl Marx: "The philosophers have only interpreted the world, the point is to change it.") Still others tend to emphasize being—quietists, mystics, existentialist philosophers, and the like. Compelling arguments can be made to opt for one or another member of the triad.

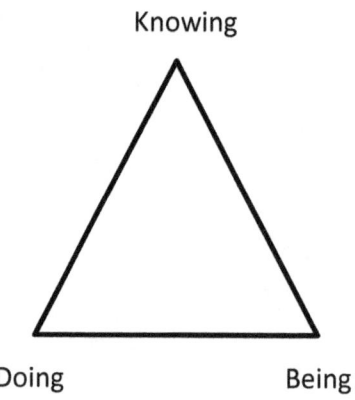

Knowing and Doctrine

A common assertion is that two of the members proceed from one—whether doing and being proceed from knowing, being and knowing proceed from doing, or knowing and doing proceed from being. Less simplistic perhaps is the view that all three members inform and shape one other in a cyclical fashion: what we know (or think we know) shapes what we do, which in turn shapes who we are, which again shapes what we know, etc.

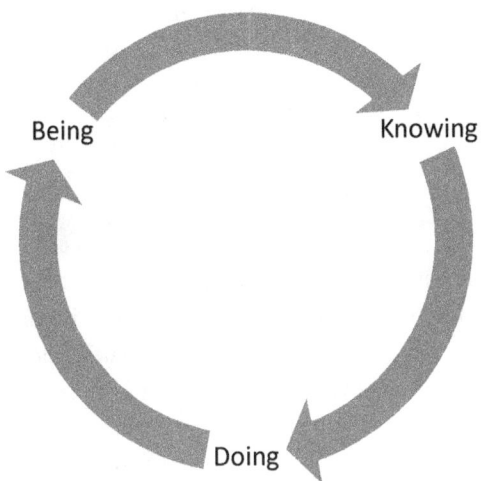

I prefer to think along these lines, for it seems that the members of the triad can only operate as an indissoluble unity. So while for instructional purposes the members may be distinguished, in reality they cannot be.

This has real implications for how we understand knowledge of God, and, more specifically, doctrine. Those who favor *knowing* typically concern themselves with orthodoxy of some sort—how should the Christian think? Those who have a higher regard for *doing* tend to be most concerned with orthopraxy—how should I as a Christian act? Those mostly concerned with *being* concern themselves with ortho-being (to coin a word)—how can the Christian develop and maintain a heart of love? One's favoring of orthodoxy, orthopraxy, or ortho-being will necessarily shape one's understanding of the knowledge of God and doctrine.

Seeking a universal ideal that fits everyone is to chase the wind, for every individual is uniquely wired and in a unique situation. All that we can do is encourage one another to find balance in the triad, which may be likened to a three-legged stool. If the ground was perfectly level the three legs of the stool would be of equal length, but the ground is far from level. Complicating things is the fact that individuals differ with respect to weight and height—factors that will determine the thickness and length of the legs. Individuals also differ with respect to the terrain that they occupy, whether it be bumpy, on a slope, on a rock, or in mud—factors that will determine the shape of the base of each leg. A single mother on welfare, a university professor during her sabbatical, a lonely shut-in at a village nursing home, a marathon runner with a broken ankle—all alike will very naturally adapt the stool to best suit them in their stations in life. The church's job is to facilitate such adaptation, to encourage the believer to find some semblance of balance, and to help them understand where they fit in the kingdom.

THE KNOWLEDGE OF GOD

The Scriptures teach that every individual has an inborn knowledge of God—an awareness that begins at birth, and that is carried on by conscience and by the observance of creation. But such knowledge is incomplete—not simply because God is infinite, but also because knowledge of God becomes distorted as individuals become increasingly absorbed both by themselves and the cares of the world. The author of Ecclesiastes has the following to say:

> He has also set eternity in the hearts of people; yet they cannot fathom what God has done from beginning to end. (Eccl 3:14)

While God has put "eternity" into the hearts of people, people are unable to understand God. Paul goes further in his teaching that the inability to understand God is largely due to sin.

> The wrath of God is being revealed from heaven against all the godlessness and wickedness of people who suppress the truth by their wickedness, since what may be known about God is plain to them, because God has made it plain to them. For since the creation of the world God's invisible qualities—his eternal power and divine nature—have been clearly seen, being understood from what has been made, so that people are without excuse. For although they knew God, they neither glorified him as God nor gave thanks to him, but their thinking became futile and their foolish hearts were darkened. . . . They did not think it worthwhile to retain the knowledge of God. (Rom 1:18–20, 28)

Knowing and Doctrine

The knowledge that here concerns Paul is ethical in nature. While God's "invisible qualities" are known by observing creation, people "suppress the truth" by their wickedness. Humanity did indeed know God, but by failing to retain such knowledge it became "darkened." Paul revisits the subject of innate knowledge of God in Romans 2:

> Indeed, when Gentiles, who do not have the law, do by nature things required by the law, they are a law for themselves, even though they do not have the law, since they show that the requirements of the law are written on their hearts, their consciences also bearing witness, and their thoughts now accusing, now even defending them. (Rom 2:14–15)

Because the requirements of the law are "written on their hearts," gentiles do "by nature" what the law requires of them.

What Paul explicitly states regarding knowledge of God and conscience is implicit through much of the Bible. That the men of Sodom and Gomorrah violated universal conscience in their treatment of Lot is assumed in the divine punishment (Gen 18–19); Abimelech's refraining from taking Sarah for himself was due to his high ethical standards (Gen 20); and the pronouncements of the prophets to the nations regularly assume that Israel shares an ethical code with the rest of humanity. A fine example in the Gospels concerns the "Good Samaritan"—whose ethical conduct greatly surpassed that of the Jewish passersby.

While knowledge of God is innate, we must remember that it is also finite. Even after we repent, even after we confess with our mouths and believe in our hearts that Jesus is Lord, and even while we long to love God with everything that we are, even then we will freely acknowledge that our knowledge of God and of things divine is finite and limited. Paul states as much in the love chapter:

> Now we see but a poor reflection as in a mirror; then we shall see face to face. Now I know in part; then I shall know fully, even as I am fully known. (1 Cor 13:12)

Paul had been swept away by the love of God in Jesus Christ. Paul enjoyed mystical union with God, even as he sought fellowship with Jesus in his sufferings. Yet Paul was aware that what he had experienced and all that he knew would be far surpassed in the next life. Paul's emphasis on the limited nature of human knowledge is unlike the concern with certainty in much of the modern world. In segments of the Evangelical world, such words as "proof," "evidence," and "certainty" have taken up an inordinate amount of space and energy. I am not suggesting that there is no room for defending the faith. As we explain the faith to the world we must seek to use its words and categories of thought. This is what Paul meant when he declared the following:

> To the Jews I became like a Jew, to win the Jews. To those under the law I became like one under the law (though I myself am not under the law), so as to win those under the law. To those not having the law I became like one not having the law (though I am not free from God's law but am under Christ's law), so as to win those not having the law. To the weak I became weak, to win the weak. I have become all things to all men so that by all possible means I might save some. (1 Cor 9:20–22)

Using the words and thought categories of the world to explain the faith is a fundamental part of living the Christian life. Indeed, the very existence of the Christian faith has always depended on this fact—for God became human to win humanity to himself. The dictum attributed to St. Augustine is here on the mark: "The Son of God became the Son of Man in order that sons of men might become sons of God." Like their Lord, Christians are called to assimilate the culture in which they exist in order to communicate the truth of God in Christ to that culture.

But we must here be very careful, for as history sadly testifies it is all too easy to allow the world's thought processes to dictate the nature of the gospel—at which point it is a case of the tail wagging the dog. Even as we seek to explain the gospel through cultural understandings, we must remember that the gospel itself stands above cultural understandings. As I pointed out earlier, Evangelicalism so bought into Enlightenment thinking that it allowed such thinking to dictate its understanding of the nature of the gospel. Insofar as the eighteenth-century church in the Western world existed in a society that embraced Enlightenment categories of thought, this church was to seek to communicate the gospel along such categories. The problem is that the eighteenth-century church (including its Evangelical wing) confused such categories with truth itself—such that, together with the doctrine of inerrancy, an emphasis was placed on certain knowledge. The church has, so it was thought, certain knowledge that God exists, that Jesus rose from the dead, that Jesus is the only way, and that the Christian ethic surpasses any other ethic. Certain knowledge of the truth of the Christian faith was only as good as demonstrating that the above claims (and many others besides) could be proven on the basis of sound reasoning. But apart from axiomatic statements like "every triangle has three sides" or "every object has mass," there is little room for certain knowledge. If ever a myth existed, it would be the myth of certitude. Because all human knowledge is finite, subject as it is to time and place, we readily concur with Paul that on this side of eternity we can only "know in part." That being the case, the communication of the gospel must at all times assume the finitude of human knowledge. This is precisely something that Evangelicalism has failed to do. The Evangelical communication of the gospel along Enlightenment categories failed even before it began, for its starting point was not "the gospel is true" but "it can be demonstrated through rational proofs that the gospel is true." Yes, the church of the eighteenth-century Enlightenment was called to communicate the gospel with Enlightenment categories in mind. Doing otherwise would have been irresponsible. Simply contending that there was little or even nothing redeemable about Enlightenment thinking (a stance that various strains of the church took), that Enlightenment thinking should be rejected entirely, is akin to the proverbial ostrich burying its head in the sand as a way of dealing with danger. But equally problematic was the approach of other churches (including much of Evangelicalism), an approach that involved the unreflective assimilation of Enlightenment categories even as such churches sought to communicate the gospel. Few sought a middle ground: no, Enlightenment thinking was not to be rejected wholesale; and no, Enlightenment thinking was not to provide the basis on which the gospel was to be presented. The middle ground might have involved replacing the rather naïve use of concepts such as certain knowledge, proof, evidence, and logic with more humble language that assumes the human condition—plausibility rather than proof, compulsion rather than demonstrability, beauty rather than observable factuality.

The gospel is not true because it can be demonstrated as being true. The gospel is, rather, self-evidently true. Because the gospel is itself a reflection of the truth of God, and because God has placed his truth into the hearts of all humanity, people know truth when they see it and hear it—unless, of course, they have allowed darkness to overcome the light that is in them. The opening of the Gospel of John teaches as much.

> In him was life, and the life was the light of all people. (John 1:4)

> The light shines in the darkness, but the darkness has not understood it. (John 1:5)

Born Again and Beyond

I noted above how the Bible assumes that people have an innate knowledge of God. Complementing this teaching is the fact that all people have "light" within them. Whatever else such light may be, it is clear from the context of the opening verses of the Gospel of John that it is the product of the Word himself, who is "the true light." While the darkness seeks to overcome the light in people, those in whom the light continues to shine know light when they see it. Such light is "full of grace and mercy." Because we know that whatever religious truth is in its fullness, it must include mercy, we say to ourselves that the gospel is true. The entire gospel is an expression of love—divine love for humanity, and love among humans. Because we long for love, we again conclude that the gospel is true. The gospel anticipates a time in which perfect harmony will exist throughout the created world. Even while discord abounds in this broken world, our hearts pine for the realization of the divine promise of universal harmony. There are many other factors that come together to help us understand truth, factors that may only be ancillary to the gospel—virtues, beauty, and tranquility. But because we participate in the true light, we know truth when we observe it. While darkness may have overcome the light in some cases, for those who have eyes to see shimmers of light dispel the darkness at every turn.

Many evangelistic conversations that I have had have convinced me that, contrary to what they might declare, people simply do not make decisions on the basis of rational explanations and logic. I remember a man telling me that because he would only believe what can be proven, and because the teaching that Jesus died for sinners cannot be proven, he would not believe in the gospel. Not long after this I saw this man reading a book that outlined belief in reincarnation, a belief that he invited me to consider. In a rather jaded fashion I told the man that I would only be too happy to believe in reincarnation if only it could first be proven. I doubt that the man noticed his inconsistency or my sarcasm. At that point I started to conclude that people believe not what is based on rational explanation but whatever satisfies their whims. This conclusion found further support in other conversations. On one occasion a friend told me that she could not believe in God because there was no reasonable basis for such a belief. In response I issued a challenge. I asked her to give me thirty minutes of her day. I told her that at the end of the allotted time she would agree that believing in the existence of God is far more plausible than believing in his non-existence. I also told her that I doubted that she would have any interest in changing her life as a consequence of learning this. My friend accepted the challenge.

Knowing and Doctrine

With pen and paper in hand, in the given thirty minutes I did a decent enough job outlining various cosmological and teleological arguments for the existence of God. When the thirty minutes came to an end I asked, "So what of it? Do you think that it is more reasonable to believe in the existence of God than in his non-existence?" My friend readily agreed that believing in God is more plausible than not believing in God. I then asked her, "How will this change your life?" Her response was pointed: "Not at all." Some years after this experience I had the honor of having breakfast with a world-renown Christian apologist. This man was brilliant. In addition to traveling from university to university to debate the existence of God, he had written many articles in academic journals as well as many books. I had read and reread several such books, which in turn led me to other books concerning apologetics and philosophy. But nothing in this man's books spoke so loudly as what he said over breakfast. At one point I asked him, "How many people that you know of have been converted as a result of your debates?" At this the apologist lowered his eyes and said in a hushed voice, "Not one." Given that I had seen time and again that people simply do not believe what is most plausible, I was not altogether shocked by the apologist's answer. His answer nevertheless surprised me, for it is difficult for me to understand how such an accomplished speaker with an unparalleled knowledge of his subject matter could fail to convert anyone over decades of debating at universities. It just does not make sense. Perhaps, however, that is the very point.

Even as it seems to be human nature to make God after one's own likeness, so cultures often operate on the assumption that their knowledge of God excels that of other cultures. The culture of Evangelicalism is no different from other cultures on this score. While the claims of Evangelicalism can certainly be challenged in this regard, I am at this point chiefly concerned with the sociology of knowledge. When a religious culture claims to know the pathway to knowledge of God, and when it implicitly teaches that any veering from this religious culture necessarily contains within it veering from the God-given way of knowing God, it follows that the individual who questions various teachings often feels that she is also questioning *the* way of knowing God. The church must then make a distinction between its expression of knowledge of God and knowledge of God more generally. From its inception, Protestantism has contended that in failing to make this distinction Roman Catholicism has effectively made itself the sole custodian of knowledge of God. Even as I readily concur, I also see that Evangelicalism has done precisely the same thing. Implicit in Evangelicalism's insistence that it knows the God-given pathway to knowledge of God is an indictment against other Christian expressions of knowledge of God. But the culture of Evangelicalism is simply not the sole custodian of knowledge of God.

I should also note that largely because Evangelicalism assumed Enlightenment understandings of the nature of knowledge, Evangelicalism as a whole has traditionally failed to make a distinction between abstract and experiential knowledge. Saying "*I know* that two plus two equals four" is very different from saying "*I know* that I like the color red." The first "*I know*" is abstract. It is based on arithmetic and has nothing whatever to do with conviction. The second "*I know*" is experiential—experience that can neither be confirmed nor denied by data outside the one who said "*I know* that I like the color red." This is not simply a matter of semantics, for Evangelicalism's failure at this point has lead to distorted faith. According to much of Evangelicalism, believers can have "certain knowledge" of their salvation. The syllogistic reasoning goes like this: (1) the Bible teaches that we can "know" that we have eternal life; (2) we "know" that whatever the Bible says is true; (3) we therefore "know" that we have eternal life. The problem with such reasoning is that when the Bible says that we "know" that we have eternal life, *it is referring to experiential (not abstract) knowledge.*

A verse that is often used in order to support the teaching that the believer can have certain knowledge of eternal life comes near the close of 1 John:

> I write these things to you who believe in the name of the Son of God so that you may *know* that you have eternal life. (1 John 5:13)

But an overview of how John uses the word "know" quickly shows us that he is here referring to experiential, not abstract knowledge. In the following two examples John uses "know" with reference to the inner testimony of the Spirit.

> And this is how we *know* that he lives in us: We *know* it by the Spirit he gave us. (1 John 3:24)

> We *know* that we live in him and he in us, because he has given us of his Spirit. (1 John 4:13)

The following examples similarly equate knowledge of salvation with love—love for others and love for God.

> We *know* that we have passed from death to life, because we love our brothers. (1 John 3:14)
>
> Whoever does not love does not *know* God, because God is love. (1 John 4:8)
>
> This is how we *know* that we love the children of God: by loving God and carrying out his commands. (1 John 5:2)

What, then, does John mean by his contention that we can "know" that we have eternal life? Simply this: because we love others as God loves us, and because the Spirit is guiding us into all truth, we have experiential knowledge of eternal life.[1]

My concern is again pragmatic. When Evangelicalism teaches that the truth of the gospel can be known by means of various arguments, Evangelicalism unwittingly sets some of its adherents up for great disillusionment. This is what happens: someone who is anxious to learn more starts to read about the weaknesses of one or another view that they have held. This may not present a problem at first: exceptions may be granted; some inconsistencies and tensions may be allowed. But as one reads more about other weaknesses, the whole edifice begins to lose shape, and it at last crumbles under its own fraudulent weight. It is here that the disillusionment is felt. Up until this point the person has placed great confidence in Evangelicalism, wholeheartedly believing that Evangelical faith is the same as Christian faith. But when this person discovers that one or another Evangelical claim is indefensible, this person concludes that the whole Christian faith must also be indefensible. The tragedy came not with discovering weaknesses in the Evangelical apparatus, but in equating Evangelical faith with Christian faith. Knowledge of God is not peculiar to any one of the hundreds of cultural expressions of Christian faith.

An Evangelical church might teach that the theory of evolution is hopelessly unscientific, and then a young person in the church goes off to university and reads Darwin's *Origin of Species* together with secondary

---

1. Similar to what we see in 1 John, the Hebrew verb *yada* ("to know") often has an experiential rather than a simply cognitive nuance. A celebrated example comes with Genesis 5:1. Whereas the NIV reads "Adam lay with his wife Eve, and she became pregnant and gave birth to Cain," the King James Version reads "Adam again *knew* his wife Eve . . . ." —which is what the Hebrew literally states. Adam's *knowledge* of his wife was intimate and experiential.

literature. After wrestling with various matters and experiencing some degree of angst, the young person concludes that Darwin—and one hundred fifty years of science after him—may well have been on to something. Again, an Evangelical church might teach that the Bible is inerrant. A young person from the church then goes to seminary only to learn that the Bible contains a host of historical incongruities, that a strictly literal understanding of the Bible is most problematic, that many of the books of the Bible are pseudonymous, and that far from the teaching that the Bible contains one voice, the messages of the Bible are as diverse as are the many authors and editors who pieced the work together over the better part of a millennium. After wrestling with various matters and experiencing some psychological turmoil, the seminarian reticently concludes that his church has unwittingly set him up for despair.

I could go on and on; and so could most anyone who had been led to believe one thing only to learn in institutions of higher education how very problematic their belief had been. I say "had" rather than "has" intentionally, for there is no returning. No doubt, students whose faith has been challenged by the academic institution may well return to their denominational roots, but more as spectators than participants, for their innocence has been lost and their trust in their church has been undermined. But the easy majority of students either find a more "liberal" place to hang their hats, or they give up on the faith question altogether. At this point the reader may well protest, for her experience has been very different: rather than the easy majority, relatively few students end up in a more "liberal" faith environment, and fewer still dispense with their faith altogether. My hunch is that this experience is based on students who attend a faith-based institution where data that may challenge Evangelical assumptions is presented only partially, not presented at all, sequestered, or kept under the watchful eye of the establishment. (I know of one such institution that stamped a great deal of its library holdings with the words "The views expressed in this book are not necessarily in keeping with Christian orthodoxy.") Another hunch is that for one reason or another such students managed to bypass any field of study that might challenge their faith.

Shortly after I started on the PhD journey, Mark Noll published a book that he entitled *The Scandal of the Evangelical Mind*. Noll's basic contention is summed up in the opening sentence: "The scandal of the evangelical mind is that there is not much of an evangelical mind." My PhD experience confirmed in a different way my own suspicions about the pursuit of truth in Evangelicalism. I had completed my Master's degree in a faith-friendly environment that did not shy away from challenges to the Evangelical mindset. I was introduced to various critical inquiries—mostly with respect to the Bible. Because the contenders for one or another perspective were often Evangelicals themselves, I assumed that Evangelicalism had a strong voice in the world of Biblical scholarship. But after only a few semesters in the PhD program, I concluded that Evangelicalism's voice was only negligible. This surprised me, for while front and center to Evangelical faith is the Bible, in the world of biblical scholarship Evangelicalism's voice is all but silent. I also found that those students who would not move from an Evangelical mindset typically opted to write their dissertations on topics that were altogether safe—topics that would not in any way challenge Evangelical thinking.

As I reflect on my own teaching within academic institutions, I see that to some extent it has been colored by the way in which I had processed my understanding of faith in light of the findings of scholarship. While this is certainly a universal experience, I nevertheless regret that I communicated my angst of soul over the chasm between what Evangelicalism teaches and what scholarship teaches. I saw truth in each, but I was at a loss when it came to explaining how such voices might be reconciled. My fear is that far from enhancing faith, I undermined it for some. All the same, I am easy on myself because I know that I came by the ability to undermine faith most honestly, for I recognize that I too am a product of my Evangelical heritage. With the very best of intentions, both my church as well as the undergraduate institution that I attended actually set me up for disillusionment. Yet I hope that I am likewise easy on them, for they are also products of their world.

CHRISTIAN DOCTRINE

In the preceding paragraphs I discussed how knowledge of God is universal, how such knowledge is finite, and how it is therefore dangerous for any Christian culture to assume that it is the principal custodian of the pathway to knowledge of God. The following discussion concerning doctrine is, in many respects, based on the foregoing discussion of knowledge of God.

Doctrine is expressed or outlined in diverse ways in the many different expressions of Christian faith. For some, doctrine is descriptive rather than simply prescriptive. A cherished dictum in this regard is *lex orandi, lex credendi* ("the law of worship is the law of belief"). Accordingly, doctrine is birthed in experience before it becomes systematized. Theology is done on one's knees before it is done in one's mind. In other expressions of Christian faith, doctrine has a prescriptive role to play. In such expressions, one may only be a member in good standing of the particular denomination or community if one concurs with the given system of doctrine. This has regularly been the role that doctrine has played in the Evangelical world, for a nearly universal feature of Evangelical organizations is a concise summary of their core doctrines—known as a statement of faith. In the following paragraphs I will discuss the problematic nature of such statements. The following is the "*World Evangelical Fellowship Statement of Faith*":

- *We believe in the Holy Scriptures as originally given by God, divinely inspired, infallible, entirely trustworthy; and the supreme authority in all matters of faith and conduct . . .*

- *One God, eternally existent in three persons, Father, Son, and Holy Spirit . . .*

- *Our Lord Jesus Christ, God manifest in the flesh, His virgin birth, His sinless human life, His divine miracles, His vicarious and atoning death, His bodily resurrection, His ascension, His mediatorial work, and His Personal return in power and glory . . .*

- *The Salvation of lost and sinful man through the shed blood of the Lord Jesus Christ by faith apart from works, and regeneration by the Holy Spirit . . .*

- *The Holy Spirit, by whose indwelling the believer is enabled to live a holy life, to witness and work for the Lord Jesus Christ . . .*

- *The Unity of the Spirit of all true believers, the Church, the Body of Christ . . .*

- *The Resurrection of both the saved and the lost; they that are saved unto the resurrection of life, they that are lost unto the resurrection of damnation.*

With the exception of the first statement (concerning the Holy Scriptures), I essentially agree with the tenets in this statement of faith. My problem is not with the particular features of this statement of faith *per se*, but with more general matters—such as what statements of faith presuppose concerning the life of faith. If statements of faith are to exist at all, let those who frame them take into consideration the following points.

The ultimate function of doctrine (and with it, statements of faith) must be that of providing life. Doctrine is the servant of the life of faith. As we study doctrine we must forever ask ourselves such questions as, "How does this doctrine further the cause of Christ in this world?" or "How does this doctrine better enable Christians to love one another?" or "How does this doctrine, together with other doctrines to which it is tied, shape the Christian's understanding of salvation?" Doctrine must never be an end in itself. Doctrine must always point beyond itself, saying, "Look to me only in order that you might have greater regard for the One in whom I exist." Regrettably, however, viewing doctrine as a means to a greater end has not always been the case. Perhaps the greatest heresy in church history is barren orthodoxy itself: an orthodoxy that concerns itself almost exclusively with how to think about faith, not about how faith is to be lived, embraced, and incarnated—an orthodoxy that lives in the clouds, that is consumed by metaphysical abstractions, and that has not allowed room for diversity. If indeed knowledge is power, then doctrine has often been the enforcer of such knowledge. Fixation on doctrine as an end in itself has left a horrific stain on the church—divisiveness and bloodshed; anathematizing, dis-fellowshipping, or even torturing "heretics" because they failed to think the right way; sanctioning grave injustices like slavery, or opposing the civil rights movement in the name of God; and demonizing "liberal secular humanist" Christians because they are thought to be unorthodox. Soren Kierkegaard's basement parable is here most apt. In this parable Kierkegaard contended that the so-called world of orthodoxy is akin to a crew building an impressive mansion . . . but choosing to live in its basement. According to the orthodox, what matters most are the specific blueprints for the doctrinal edifice, not actually choosing to live in the edifice itself. In saying this I am not in any way dismissing doctrine, for I am only too aware that it can be a source of great life. My concern is that love of doctrine does not replace love of God and neighbor.

Statements of faith typically confuse faith with doctrine. The two are not the same. Faith is subjective and interior. It is all about personal trust in a personal God in the context of a faith community. Faith concerns encountering, or being encountered, by God. Doctrine is very different from faith. Doctrine is largely objective and exterior from the individual. Together with other matters, doctrine seeks to inform us of the nature of

God, God's redemption of humanity through the person and work of Jesus Christ, the nature of the church, and the end and goal of history. At its best, doctrine can inform faith, but it can never replace it. "Statement of faith" is thus a misnomer, for such statements concern systems of doctrine that one may agree or disagree with at the cognitive level. One can have a great knowledge of doctrine, but have no faith whatsoever. We might here think of some members of the religious establishment, not unlike some Pharisees of old, whose knowledge of doctrine is profound but whose simple trust in God is all but absent. So also, one may have great faith while only knowing little doctrine. We might think of a mentally challenged person, or that gentile centurion of whom Jesus said, "I have not found such great faith even in Israel" (Luke 7:9). Faith and doctrine are not the same.

Statements of faith should also be consistent with the way in which God has revealed himself to humanity through the Bible. Stated otherwise, doctrinal formulations ought to be consistent with the nature of biblical revelation itself. It is here instructive that while statements of faith are altogether systematic, the Bible itself simply does not outline the life of faith in a systematic fashion. The Bible contains a host of genres—stories, proverbs, poetry, parables, and the like. The Bible simply *never* presents faith in a systematic fashion. The very nature of a statement of faith is not consistent with the way in which God has revealed himself through Scripture. Statements of faith concern cognitive agreement with systems of thought—systems that have been sanctioned by one religious establishment or another.

Consistent with the fact that the statement of faith genre is foreign to biblical genres, statements of faith should be story-like—for that is precisely how the faith has been explained and experienced through the millennia. Living in a storied world is integral to the human condition. Our interpretations of the past, our understandings of the present, and our anticipations for the future are all profoundly shaped by stories—be they folk tales, national dreams, Scripture, or the worldviews that we assume. Storied worlds captivate individuals and nations, they determine how other stories are interpreted, and they themselves are the product of earlier stories that have organized and defined a myriad of data. Given that stories (rather than rational systems of thought) are part of what it means to be human, given that God himself has wired all humanity in this way, and given that biblical revelation comes to us as a story, it seems to me that statements of faith should also be story-like. It was in a story-like manner that people in the Old Testament outlined their faith. Here are two examples.

> In the future, when your son asks you, "What is the meaning of the stipulations, decrees and laws the Lord our God has commanded you?" tell him: "We were slaves of Pharaoh in Egypt, but the Lord brought us out of Egypt with a mighty hand. Before our eyes the Lord sent miraculous signs and wonders—great and terrible—upon Egypt and Pharaoh and his whole household. But he brought us out from there to bring us in and give us the land that he promised on oath to our forefathers." (Deut 6:20–23)

> Then you shall declare before the Lord your God: "My father was a wandering Aramean, and he went down into Egypt with a few people and lived there and became a great nation, powerful and numerous. But the Egyptians mistreated us and made us suffer, putting us to hard labor. Then we cried out to the Lord, the God of our fathers, and the Lord heard our voice and saw our misery, toil and oppression. So the Lord brought us out of Egypt with a mighty hand and an outstretched arm, with great terror and with miraculous signs and wonders. He brought us to this place and gave us this land, a land flowing with milk and honey; and now I bring the firstfruits of the soil that you, O Lord, have given me." (Deut 26:5–10)

The reader will note that there is great narrative correspondence between the two passages. Were we to look at the several other examples of such confessions we would also observe such correspondence, which is due to ancient Israel's understanding of itself and its relation to God's work with it through history—not through an abstract system of rational thought. The God of Abraham, Isaac, and Jacob is not the god of Socrates, Plotinus, and Sartre. The context in which the second example appears is one of worship—the confession is made as the worshipper presents an offering to the priest in the temple. Liturgical churches similarly express their faith in story-like terms as they celebrate communion, in which the person leading the communion service recounts the high points of the biblical story, and during which the gathered community might say something like "Christ has died, Christ is risen, Christ will come again."

Consistent with the conviction that statements of faith ought to be story-like, they should also focus on what it means to be an individual in community before God. Jesus never invited people to adhere to a system of thought. Every time that Jesus presented the good news to people, he did so in an individualized manner. To Nicodemus he said one thing, to Zaccheus another, to the thief on the cross still another. Jesus told the rich young man that his riches impeded him from entering the kingdom. To religious leaders, Jesus spoke of hypocrisy and being judgmental. At every turn Jesus tailor-made the good news to the needs of the people that he addressed. Apart from such general teachings that people need to turn from self toward God, or be merciful to others even as God has been merciful to them, from the standpoint of Jesus there was no such thing as a one-size-fits-all presentation of the gospel. The shades that the good news comes in are as diverse as is the human population—age, ethnicity, gender, life experience, education, level of income, etc.

As it is, statements of faith tend to be abstract systems of thought. We need to move from abstraction to actualization in all doctrines. Doctrines are only true in the full sense when they are embodied, when they are lived, when they are embraced by believers. Seeking to explain the gospel simply along the lines of a cognitive framework is to distort the gospel at its most fundamental level, for the gospel involves the real God becoming a real man, the real Spirit taking on real flesh in this real world. It is the ancient Greeks, the Platonists, and the Gnostics who made a wild differentiation between the world of thought and the world of reality. But Christians, those who believe that Spirit and flesh became indivisibly one in Jesus, must not make such a distinction. Doctrine must be lived in this real world before it is complete; for it to be transformative, doctrine cannot exist in a disembodied state. There is a tremendous difference between believing in the Triune God at an abstract level and actually living for the Triune God. (I am here reminded of Thomas à Kempis's famous statement: "What does it profit one to discourse profoundly on the doctrine of the Trinity, but be void of humility, and thereby displease the Trinity?") Believing in Jesus is not the same as loving him. Concurring that Jesus did indeed die for sinners is not the same as embracing this truth. Believing in the bodily resurrection of Christ is not the same thing as its necessary outworking—rising to new life in Christ. Having a belief about the second coming and the eternal state is not the same as allowing hope in the future restoration transform one's present existence. Believing the abstraction that God is love only has meaning when the belief becomes physical, when help is given to the needy, when encouragement is given to the downhearted. The love of God does not exist outside of physical expressions of such love.

Statements of faith also ought to celebrate unity in the midst of diversity. As it is, statements of faith have had exclusionary roles to play. Implicit in them is the declaration, "If you wish to be one with us, you must think

Knowing and Doctrine

in these categories." Such a declaration is simply antithetical to Christian faith—even as Paul teaches in 1 Corinthians. Paul goes to great lengths in 1 Corinthians to underline the fact that mature faith in Christ expresses itself in the acknowledgement that while the body of Christ is one, it is nevertheless made up of many parts. Close to the beginning of 1 Corinthians Paul bemoans the fact that there were so many cliques within the church at Corinth.

> I appeal to you, brothers and sisters, in the name of our Lord Jesus Christ, that all of you agree with one another so that there may be no divisions among you and that you may be perfectly united in mind and thought. My brothers and sisters, some from Chloe's household have informed me that there are quarrels among you. What I mean is this: One of you says, "I follow Paul"; another, "I follow Apollos"; another, "I follow Cephas"; still another, "I follow Christ." (1 Cor 1:10–12)

The fact that this complaint appears close to the beginning of the letter tells the reader that much of what follows will concern this very subject—this was a standard practice of Paul (and of Greek letter writing more generally). At the beginning of chapter three Paul asserts that all such partisanship has no place in the life of faith.

> Brothers and sisters, I could not address you as spiritual but as worldly—mere infants in Christ. I gave you milk, not solid food, for you were not yet ready for it. Indeed, you are still not ready. You are still worldly. For since there is jealousy and quarreling among you, are you not worldly? Are you not acting like mere people? For when one says, "I follow Paul," and another, "I follow Apollos," are you not mere people? (1 Cor 3:1–4)

In chapters 8 and 10 Paul chastises those in the church at Corinth who deliberately offended others in the church who refused to eat meat that had been sacrificed to idols by eating such meat—the real offense was not eating such meat, but failing to appreciate the beliefs of some in the church. Unity trumps differences of belief. In chapter 12 Paul contends that "the body is a unit, though it is made up of many parts; and though all its parts are many, they form one body" (1 Cor 12:12). It is altogether destructive for one part of the body to think that it is more valuable than any other part, for each part needs the others for its own survival. The "body" is the church, the primary instrument through which Jesus works in this world. The "parts" of the body, while very different from one another, must recognize the importance of one other if they wish to be healthy parts of the body. Again, any church's faithfulness to Christ is directly tied to its recognition that other churches are equal members of Christ's body. There is simply no room for exclusivity, for creating a statement of faith that fails to recognize the God-givenness of different members who similarly confess that Jesus is Lord.

Statements of faith also ought to leave room for mystery. Given that they are grounded in an Enlightenment worldview, it comes as no surprise that little, if any room is given for mystery. Yet as I noted above, even while Paul presumably had an unmatched knowledge both of the Hebrew Scriptures and the Christian faith, he could readily confess that all human knowledge of eternity is but a "poor reflection," only a "knowing in part." Consistent with this, New Testament authors often used the word "mystery" with reference to the hitherto secret work of God that has now been made known.

> Now to him who is able to establish you by my gospel and the proclamation of Jesus Christ, according to the revelation of the *mystery* hidden for long ages past, but now revealed and made known through the prophetic writings by the command of the eternal God, so that all nations might believe and obey him—to the only wise God be glory forever through Jesus Christ! Amen. (Rom 16:25–27)

> . . . the *mystery* that has been kept hidden for ages and generations, but is now disclosed to the saints. To them God has chosen to make known among the Gentiles the glorious riches of this *mystery*, which is Christ in you, the hope of glory. (Col 1:26–27)

> Beyond all question, the *mystery* of our religion is great: He appeared in a body, was vindicated by the Spirit, was seen by angels, was preached among the nations, was believed on in the world, was taken up in glory. (1 Tim 3:16)[2]

The Christian faith is the unfolding of the mystery of God's plan of salvation for humanity. The divine election of Israel, the incarnation of the Word, the Christ story, the acceptance of the gospel by the Gentiles, the resurrection of the dead, the return of Christ, and the restoration of all things—all such

---

2. Following the New Revised Standard Version, I think that "our religion" is a more suitable rendering of *eusebeia* than the more literal rendering of "godliness" (NIV), which in popular English parlance often has a "holier-than-thou" nuance.

Knowing and Doctrine

truths unpack the "mystery" of God. Christians are people who embrace and find their own identity in such mysteries. Again, statements of faith fall short of biblical faith.

I am here reminded of a story concerning St. Thomas Aquinas, one of the most influential theologians of all time. Before he had completed his chief work, his *Summa Theologica*, Aquinas is said to have had a vision that so overwhelmed him that he did not finish writing. In response to a question regarding his failure to continue writing, Aquinas said, "All that I have written seems to me so much straw after the things that have been revealed to me." Aquinas's statement is similar to that of other theologians who have taught that even as they feel compelled to talk about God, they feel compelled not to talk about God—simply because positive statements about God can never do justice to who God really is. The end or ultimate goal of all God-talk is to bring us to ineffable mystery, awe, and silence.

Statements of faith also ought to leave room for change over time. I am not here suggesting in the least that the truth of God changes. "Jesus Christ is the same yesterday, today, and forever" (Heb 13:8). No, truth does not change; but categories of faithful human thought do, and the world definitely does. And just as the church nuances and tailor-makes the eternal truth of the gospel to the ever-changing needs of society, so Evangelicalism ought to adapt its statements of faith. In liturgical churches (Roman Catholic, Orthodox, Lutheran, Anglican, etc.), the Apostles' Creed or the Nicene Creed have a similar function to statements of faith in the Evangelical world. Positively, such creeds appear not as metaphysical abstractions with no immediate bearing on reality, for the creeds are used in the context of worship. Negatively, however, unless the creeds are carefully reflected upon, they have little bearing on how to live the Christian life. To begin with, the creeds jump from the virgin birth of Jesus to his crucifixion—not even pausing to acknowledge that Jesus might have said something worthwhile! I am aware that the creeds do so because in the early centuries (in which the creeds were formulated), the church fought various heresies regarding the nature of Christ and the nature of God. But those controversies have been fought. New controversies that are no less dangerous to apostolic faith now confront the church—modernity, secularism, consumerism, relativism, and religious pluralism. And other controversies will certainly become front-and-center in the years to come. In my mind, the liturgical churches therefore err with their use of the creeds—for while everything written in the creeds may well be true, failing to nuance the creeds in accordance with the immediate needs of both church and society is irresponsible. What I am here saying about the function of creeds in liturgical churches may be readily applied to the function of statements of faith in Evangelicalism—for statements of faith implicitly teach Evangelical believers that what really matters is unchanging doctrine.

The closest thing to a statement of faith in the New Testament is the simple confession *Kurios Iēsous*, "Jesus is Lord" (1 Cor 12:3). This confession was tremendously counter-cultural insofar as it implicitly challenged the common view that "Caesar is Lord." This confession perhaps had yet more force in the Jewish mind, for it equated Jesus with Yahweh ("*Kurios*" of the Greek Old Testament) the God of Israel. This confession, moreover, was typically made in a setting of worship—in a hymn perhaps, or at a baptism. As the confession was made, the concern of the community was devotion to King Jesus, not mental assent to a system of thought that purports to outline the unchanging faith. In whatever ethnic context the confession was made, it was scandalous in the extreme: Jesus of Nazareth, not Caesar of Rome, is Lord of all; and together with the God of Abraham, Isaac, and Jacob, Lord Jesus is ushering in the eternal kingdom. The confession is profound in its simplicity. It acknowledges that Jesus is one with God, even as it expresses a longing not for the *pax* of Rome, but for the eternal kingdom that comes to earth with the Prince of Peace.

Chapter Four

The Gospel and the Cross

IN THE PRECEDING CHAPTER I discussed how Evangelicalism's use and understanding of *knowing* is altogether wanting—both as it relates to knowledge of God and to doctrine. In this chapter I will discuss that while Evangelicalism's emphasis on *doing* is commendable, its understanding of *being* is poor. Evangelicalism shines most of all in the area of doing, more specifically with regard to the "great commission." Jesus said the following prior to his ascension:

> All authority in heaven and on earth has been given to me. Therefore go and make disciples of all nations, baptizing them in the name of the Father and of the Son and of the Holy Spirit, and teaching them to obey everything I have commanded you. (Matt 28:18–20)

While the great commission of Jesus has received some attention over the last two millennia, few groups within Christianity have sought to champion the cause of spreading the gospel like Evangelicalism has. There are now innumerable missionary agencies in the world, most of which have been started by Evangelical Christians; and even as Christianity seems to have fallen out of favor in the Western world, the developing world has picked up the baton of evangelizing the world—even sending missionaries to the so-called developed world.

In more recent times Evangelicalism has also coupled its emphasis on obedience to the great commission with obedience to "the great command":

> A new command I give you: Love one another. As I have loved you, so you must love one another. (John 13:34)

Evangelical organizations like World Vision, Samaritan's Purse, thousands of soup kitchens in inner cities, and a host of other organizations besides, have arisen as beautiful expressions of God's love—organizations whose objective is to feed the hungry, to assist the poor, to intervene in natural calamities, to treat sickness, and to alleviate suffering. All such doing is simply tremendous.

THE GOSPEL

I stated above that "few groups within Christianity have sought to champion the cause of spreading the gospel like Evangelicalism has." I need to address this matter with more attention. Yes, Evangelicalism has "sought" to champion the gospel, but its understanding of the nature of the gospel itself is often most troublesome, even unscriptural. The Evangelical understanding of the gospel has been cast, not so much by the Bible, but by Luther's understanding of the doctrine of justification by faith. In the early sixteenth century, Luther contended that one is justified before God not on the basis of good works but as a consequence of "faith alone" in the atoning sacrifice of Jesus Christ. This teaching became central to Protestantism, and with it, Evangelicalism. In the Evangelical mind, the doctrine of justification by faith is, for all intents and purposes, equivalent to the gospel itself.

The teaching that salvation does not come as a consequence of good works but because of faith in the work of Christ is to be celebrated. All the same, *by "works" Paul was often referring not to good works in general, but the works of the law, that is obedience to specific statutes of Moses*—particularly, statutes concerning circumcision or dietary matters. Paul's concern was to emphasize that no works of the law of Moses can bring salvation. Evangelicalism's assumption that "works" means "good works" rather than "works of the law" is based on a misreading of Paul. No, good works by themselves will not save anyone, but true faith in the work of Christ will *necessarily* generate good works. Where good works are absent, there is simply no real faith in Christ.

By limiting the gospel to a misreading of Paul's teaching concerning the subject of faith vs. works, Evangelicalism has unintentionally downplayed the fact that the gospel also concerns the salvation of everything in God's world—political landscapes, worldviews, ethics, the environment, the poor, education, laws, individual relationship to community, and even the very cosmos itself. Yes, in the past centuries Evangelicalism has worked tirelessly to promote the teaching that Christ alone can save the sinner. I celebrate this; but it must be understood that Christ dying to save sinners is not the whole gospel. For it to be properly appreciated, the redemption of the individual must be seen in the greater context of the redemption of the entire created order.

A related teaching of Luther that Evangelicalism has unreflectively subscribed to concerns the term *righteousness*. Both the sixteenth-century Protestant reformers as well as their Roman Catholic "adversaries" (that is how the parties thought of one another) made a distinction between "imputed" and "imparted" righteousness. Imputed righteousness, which was also referred to as "reckoned" righteousness, amounts to a legal transaction between God and the sinner, in which God's perfect righteousness is exchanged for the individual's sinfulness. The basis of this exchange was the crucifixion of Jesus—upon whom all the sins of the world were placed. The individual who has faith in Jesus Christ, even though he is a sinner, is regarded as being completely righteous before God, who now sees the sinner not as he is but through the lens of the righteousness of Jesus. This is imputed righteousness. Imparted righteousness, on the other hand, is an actualized righteousness. The believer has faith that she will grow in the fruits of the Spirit and all godliness because the Holy Spirit enables her to do so. Such righteousness is indicative of the true work of God in the believer's life, and as such it is key to salvation. This is imparted righteousness. The question in many sixteenth-century disputes was whether it was imputed or imparted righteousness that saves.

Biblical scholars and theologians have subsequently concluded that making a distinction between imputed and imparted righteousness is contrary to what the New Testament teaches (particularly in Romans and Galatians). The reasoning behind this conclusion is that Paul's discussions concerning imputed and imparted righteousness are altogether inseparable from one another. It is entirely alien to Pauline thinking that one can exist without the other—for justification, sanctification, and glorification are all mixed up with one another. Here are two examples.

> But you were *washed*, you were *sanctified*, you were *justified* in the name of the Lord Jesus Christ and by the Spirit of our God. (1 Cor 6:11)

> And those he *predestined*, he also *called*; those he *called*, he also *justified*; those he *justified*, he also *glorified* (Rom 8:30).

Paul's use of the term *righteousness* was largely based on how the Old Testament uses this term. Someone was righteous if they acted faithfully toward an agreement that they had made with another person. The same is true of God—God is righteous insofar as he is faithful to his promise to prosper both humanity and all of creation (a promise that is implicit in the very act of creation). Here is an example from the Psalms.

> Your love, O Lord, reaches to the heavens, your faithfulness to the skies. Your *righteousness* is like the mighty mountains, your justice like the great deep. O Lord, you preserve both man and beast. How priceless is your unfailing love! Both high and low among men find refuge in the shadow of your wings. They feast on the abundance of your house; you give them drink from your river of delights. For with you is the fountain of life; in your light we see light. Continue your love to those who know you, your *righteousness* to the upright in heart. (Ps 36:5–10)

The term *righteousness* here appears in tandem with such terms as *unfailing love* and *faithfulness*. In this instance, together with many others besides, the righteousness of God concerns God's faithfulness towards his eternal promise to want the best for creation. In other passages, divine righteousness language is used together with language that is used elsewhere with reference to a divine covenant.

> I proclaim *righteousness* in the great assembly; I do not seal my lips, as you know, O Lord. I do not hide your *righteousness* in my heart; I speak of your faithfulness and salvation. I do not conceal your love and your truth from the great assembly. Do not withhold your mercy from me, O Lord; may your love and your truth always protect me. (Ps 40:9–11)

We here read that the Psalmist proclaims the righteousness of God to the worshipping community, a righteousness that is one with God's "faithfulness," "salvation," "love," "truth," and "mercy"—language that is used elsewhere with reference to the very reason that God keeps covenant with Israel. Left to itself, Israel (and all humanity) is entirely unable to maintain covenant faithfulness with God. The covenant can only stay intact if it is based on God's mercy, for humanity is forever wayward and self-seeking. It is for this reason that the covenant is often referred to as the "covenant of love" (e.g., Deut 7:9, 12). The righteousness of God is made manifest precisely at this point. God is righteous insofar as he is forever faithful to maintaining covenant—even irrespective of humanity's unrighteousness. Consistent with the meaning of the term *righteousness* in the Old Testament, Paul often used this term with reference to the way in which God remains faithful to the covenant that he has made with humanity.

For centuries now, one of Protestantism's favorite texts used in support of imputed righteousness has been 2 Cor 5:21.

> God made him who had no sin to be sin for us, so that in him we might become the righteousness of God.

With the Protestant Reformers, Evangelicalism has found in this passage a clear and concise teaching of imputed righteousness: simply by having faith in Jesus Christ (whom God made to be "sin for us" while he was on the cross), the believer exchanges his sin for the very "righteousness of God." But a more reflective look at this passage in its immediate context quickly tells us that this celebrated passage has nothing whatever to do with imputed righteousness. Let us take a look, then, at the greater context in which this passage appears.

> All this is from God, who reconciled us to himself through Christ and gave us the ministry of reconciliation: that God was reconciling the world to himself in Christ, not counting people's sins against them. And he has committed to us the message of reconciliation. We are therefore Christ's ambassadors, as though God were making his appeal through us. We implore you on Christ's behalf: Be reconciled to God. God made him who had no sin to be sin for us, so that in him we might become the righteousness of God. (2 Cor 5:17–21)

The pivotal concept in this passage concerns the "message of reconciliation": God "reconciled" believers to himself through Christ; God in turn gave believers the "ministry of reconciliation"—committing to them the "message of reconciliation"—thus making believers Christ's "ambassadors." It is with regard to this ministry of reconciliation that the given verse is to be understood: consistent with Paul's use of the term *righteousness* elsewhere, Paul's declaration that "we might become the righteousness of God" is all about how God is faithful to the covenant. More specifically, God is in the process of fulfilling his plan for the salvation of humanity by committing "the message of reconciliation" to believers. As such, the concluding phrase "righteousness of God" concerns God's covenant faithfulness:

believers become "the righteousness of God" insofar as they are ambassadors of his truth. I am not here seeking to undermine the doctrine of imputed righteousness. I only wish to underline the point that interpreting 2 Corinthians 5:21 along such lines is contrary to the context in which it appears.

As with the word "righteousness," understanding what the Greek term *euangelion* (pronounced "oo-an-gellion") means must be front and center to any discussion concerning Evangelicalism. Indeed, the English term "evangelical" is taken from *euangelion*—the term that is variously translated as "good news" or "gospel." Prior to discussing what the term *euangelion* means in the New Testament, at this point I will discuss what the term means in the Old Testament.

The Hebrew equivalent of the Greek term *euangelion* is *bsarah*. In the Old Testament the verb *basar* (pronounced "ba-sar," "to proclaim good news") often refers to a herald's message. Upon learning of the victory of his army over another army, the herald proclaims to his people the news that the enemy had been defeated. After the Philistines, for example, had killed Saul and his sons on Mount Gilboa, "they sent messengers throughout the land of the Philistines *to proclaim the good news*" (1 Sam 31:9). In later Old Testament literature, words associated with the verb *basar* were applied to the new age that God was to bring about, as is the case with the following passage from Isaiah.

> How beautiful on the mountains are the feet of those who bring *good news*, who proclaim peace, who bring *good tidings*, who proclaim salvation, who say to Zion, "Your God reigns!" Listen! Your watchmen lift up their voices; together they shout for joy. When the Lord returns to Zion, they will see it with their own eyes. Burst into songs of joy together, you ruins of Jerusalem, for the Lord has comforted his people, he has redeemed Jerusalem. The Lord will lay bare his holy arm in the sight of all the nations, and all the ends of the earth will see the salvation of our God. (Isa 52:7–10)

Consistent with the use of the term *bsarah* elsewhere, the imagery here involves a herald coming to Jerusalem to proclaim the news that the Lord had defeated his foes in battle. The Lord will continue to defeat those who oppose his righteous rule, such that "all the ends of the earth" will witness his work. Significant for our purposes, the *bsarah* in the given passage concerns the rebuilding of the city of Jerusalem. While Jerusalem had been ravaged time and again by great nations, while Babylon had exiled Jerusalem's inhabitants and burned down the temple, the promise was that the new age would begin with the LORD defeating all those who opposed Jerusalem. As with the given example, throughout the Old Testament "good news" has earthy overtones. The term is used with reference to victory over oppressing forces, deliverance from poverty, and release of the imprisoned. There is not a single instance in which *bsarah* strictly concerns deliverance from personal sin or having a personal relationship with God.

We turn, now, to a discussion of the Greek equivalent of *bsarah* in ancient Roman literature—the Greek term *euangelion*. To understand the meaning of *euangelion* in such literature, one must do so in light of how the Emperor was understood. Among other titles, in the Roman world the Emperor was thought of as lord, savior, god, deliverer, and miracle worker. In his overview of the use of the term *euangelion* in ancient Roman literature, Friedrich Hauk could state the following:

> The ruler is divine by nature. His power extends to men, to animals, to the earth and to the sea. Nature belongs to him; wind and waves are subject to him. He works miracles and heals men. He is the saviour of the world who also redeems individuals from their difficulties.... He has appeared on earth as a deity in human form. He is the protective god of the state. His appearance is the cause of good fortune to the whole kingdom. Extraordinary signs accompany the course of his life. They proclaim the birth of the ruler of the world. A comet appears at his accession, and at his death signs in heaven declare his assumption into the ranks of the gods.... The emperor is more than a common man.[1]

Understandably, early Christians had great difficulty with viewing the Emperor along such lines. Jesus, not Caesar, is the Lord, the Savior, and God become human; and it is in Jesus, not Caesar that *euangelion* to humanity has come. Jesus, not Caesar, is the creator and sustainer of the cosmos. It is in Jesus, not Caesar, that lasting peace has come. The problem that Christians had with the typical understanding of the Emperor was the precise inverse of the problem that the Romans had with the Christians. The Christians could not confess that Caesar is Lord. They applied prerogatives that belonged only to Caesar to Jesus. In the eyes of Rome, doing so was treasonous, even "atheistic." Throughout the empire, Christians paid the price for such irreligion—from slurs in the marketplace to martyrdom in the coliseum. In spite of harsh persecution, many early Christians did not

---

1. Friedrich Hauk, *euangelion,* in ed. Gehrad Kittel, *Theological Dictionary of the New Testament* (Grand Rapids: Eerdmans, 1964), 724-25.

seem to be fazed. An indication of such tenacity in the face of cruel opposition was the Christians' endless praise of Jesus, even applying titles that had been given to Caesar to Jesus—who alone is "Kings of kings and Lord of lords" (Rev 19:16).

It is in this historical milieu that the term *euangelion* must be understood. The first hearers of the proclamation of Jesus would have understood *euangelion* as being a challenge to the common thinking that the *euangelion* only comes from Caesar. Here is another statement from Hauk:

> What [the Emperor] says is a divine act and implies good and salvation for men. He proclaims *euangelia* [the plural of *euangelion*] through his appearance . . . . Other *euangelia* follow . . . . Joy and rejoicing come with the news . . . . Doom is feared because the gods have withdrawn from the earth. Then suddenly there rings out the news that the saviour is born, that he has mounted the throne, that a new era dawns for the whole world. This *euangelion* is celebrated with offerings and yearly festivals. All cherished hopes are exceeded. The world has taken on a new appearance.[2]

According to Roman imperial literature, the *euangelion* is that the Emperor will inaugurate a new age in which the peace and prosperity of Rome will become known throughout the world. Far from simply referring to spiritual salvation, such *euangelia* from the Emperor concerns material prosperity, citizenship rights, and protection from barbarians. How, we might ask, is this similar to or dissimilar from Jesus's understanding of the *euangelion*? Let us here reflect on a few passages. The first passage that we will consider appears at the commencement of Jesus's ministry:

> He went to Nazareth, where he had been brought up, and on the Sabbath day he went into the synagogue, as was his custom. And he stood up to read. The scroll of the prophet Isaiah was handed to him. Unrolling it, he found the place where it is written: "The Spirit of the Lord is on me, because he has anointed me to preach *euangelion* to the poor. He has sent me to proclaim freedom for the prisoners and recovery of sight for the blind, to release the oppressed, to proclaim the year of the Lord's favor." Then he rolled up the scroll, gave it back to the attendant and sat down. The eyes of everyone in the synagogue were fastened on him, and he began by saying to them, "Today this scripture is fulfilled in your hearing." All spoke well of him and were amazed at the gracious words that came from his lips. "Isn't this Joseph's son?" they asked. Jesus

2. Ibid., 725.

The Gospel and the Cross

said to them, "Surely you will quote this proverb to me: 'Physician, heal yourself! Do here in your hometown what we have heard that you did in Capernaum.'" "I tell you the truth," he continued, "no prophet is accepted in his hometown. I assure you that there were many widows in Israel in Elijah's time, when the sky was shut for three and a half years and there was a severe famine throughout the land. Yet Elijah was not sent to any of them, but to a widow in Zarephath in the region of Sidon. And there were many in Israel with leprosy in the time of Elisha the prophet, yet not one of them was cleansed—only Naaman the Syrian." All the people in the synagogue were furious when they heard this. They got up, drove him out of the town, and took him to the brow of the hill on which the town was built, in order to throw him down the cliff. But he walked right through the crowd and went on his way. (Luke 4:16–21, 28–30)

This passage (together with the rest of Jesus's ministry) needs to be interpreted in light of the messianic fervor among the Jewish populous of the first century. While there were many competing views of who the messiah would be and what the messiah would do—conjectures concerning his relationship to "the suffering servant," his understanding of the traditions of the fathers, and his perspective on temple worship, the following description of the messiah and his work was not atypical. To begin with, the term *messiah* was *never* used with reference to someone who would only deliver people from their sins. The messiah was to deliver the Jews, rather, from the hated Roman oppressors. Following such deliverance, the messiah would secure the borders of Israel and reinstitute pure worship in the temple. Gentiles from surrounding nations would be converted to the Jewish faith, and a new age would dawn—an age in which righteousness would flourish, perfect peace would abound, and everyone would live "under their own vine and fig tree." In a word, the new age that the messiah would usher in was a new Eden. It concerned not a heavenly hereafter but the land of Israel and its influence on the rest of the physical world. The new age had ramifications for politics, economics, education, and welfare. There was nothing in the world that would not be transformed by the new age. The passage that Jesus read in the synagogue in Nazareth on that Sabbath day was Isaiah 61:1–2, a passage that was understood by all to be referring to the messiah and to the new age that would come with him.

We must explain the bizarre about-face of the people: immediately after Jesus read and interpreted the messianic passage, the people spoke highly of him; but when Jesus suggested that the gentiles would be more receptive of the kingdom of God than they themselves, the people of Nazareth became "furious" and sought to cast Jesus off the cliff. The people of Nazareth rejected Jesus not because he said that the new age (with all its earthy transformations) was at hand, but simply because he told them that gentiles would be more receptive of the messianic reign than they themselves. That is to say, the people's fury toward Jesus was not at all based on his understanding of the nature of the *euangelion* as something that pertained to the complete reorganization of this world. The *euangelion* of Jesus would bring hope to economically poor and politically oppressed people. The *euangelion* of Jesus was that true justice would reign, and that the political landscape would be forever changed—such that eternal "peace on earth" would ensue. Entirely consistent with how ancient Roman literature as well as the Old Testament used *euangelion* and *bsarah*, then, Jesus's use of the term *euangelion* thus had overtly political overtones. This is very different from the typical Evangelical understanding of *euangelion*, which is all about deliverance from personal sin. No doubt, understandings of the *euangelion* both in Roman literature and in the gospel included the subject of deliverance from sin, but for both parties the *euangelion* had much broader connotations than this.

Another passage that shows that Jesus's understanding of the *euangelion* is not simply about spiritual deliverance is found in Matthew 11.

> When John heard in prison what Christ was doing, he sent his disciples to ask him, "Are you the one who was to come, or should we expect someone else?" Jesus replied, "Go back and report to John what you hear and see: The blind receive sight, the lame walk, those who have leprosy are cured, the deaf hear, the dead are raised, and the *euangelion* is preached to the poor." (Matt 11:2–5)

In this text we find that John the Baptist sent his disciples to ask Jesus if he was the promised messiah. Rather than providing a yes or no answer, Jesus responded by quoting passages in Isaiah that were interpreted as referring to the nature of the messianic reign. As with the example from Luke 4, there is nothing in this case that suggests that Jesus's understanding of the *euangelion* was about having a personal relationship with God. Once again, for Jesus the *euangelion* is much more than that, for it concerns divine healings and hope for the poor—characteristics of the new age.

I have suggested, then, that *euangelion* has earthy overtones. The term never strictly refers to spiritual salvation. The meaning of *euangelion* has thus been hijacked by Evangelicalism, for throughout its existence, Evangelicalism on the whole has insisted that the *euangelion* concerns spiritual salvation—more specifically, Evangelicalism's (errant) understanding of Paul's teaching of justification by grace through faith alone. No doubt, the gospel includes spiritual salvation. As someone who believes that "Jesus died for sinners," I celebrate this. Yes, the believer is forgiven for their sins on the basis of "the blood of the spotless Lamb of God that was shed at cavalry" some two millennia ago. About this life-changing truth I have no question whatever. But this truth is simply not the whole gospel, for the gospel concerns the salvation of all existence—not simply individual souls.

THE CROSS

We turn, now, to a discussion of the cross. Because the subjects of the gospel and the cross are interrelated, it comes as no surprise that Evangelicalism's failure to understand the gospel is tied to its failure to understand the cross. If the most central tenet of the Evangelical expression of faith concerns Scripture, a close second would be its understanding of the effects of the crucifixion. As far as it goes, this is a great point to emphasize. Yet my criticism of Evangelicalism concerns *how* the message of the cross is central to the gospel. I will limit the discussion to one passage of Scripture.

> 15 He is the image of the invisible God, the firstborn over all creation. 16 For by him *all things* were created: things in heaven and on earth, visible and invisible, whether thrones or powers or rulers or authorities; *all things* were created by him and for him. 17 He is before *all things*, and in him *all things* hold together. 18 And he is the head of the body, the church; he is the beginning and the firstborn from among the dead, so that in *everything* he might have the supremacy. 19 For God was pleased to have all his fullness dwell in him, 20 and through him to reconcile to himself *all things*, whether things on earth or things in heaven, by making peace through his blood, shed on the cross. (Col 1:15–20)

Important for our purposes is the fact that the author of the above passage states that through the cross God reconciled all things to himself. The passage tells us that "all things" were created by Christ and for Christ (v. 16), that he is before "all things" (v. 17), that in him "all things" hold together (v. 17), in "everything" he has the supremacy (v. 18), and that God reconciled "all things" through him (v. 20). The repeated use of "all things" includes "things in heaven and on earth" (v. 15). God brought reconciliation of all existence, things "visible and invisible" (v. 15) to himself through the cross (v. 20). The cross is the instrument of God's salvation for the entire cosmos. Thinking that the cross only concerns the redemption of humanity before God is therefore incomplete. (The specific redemption of individuals by means of the cross is not even explicitly mentioned in this passage!) Humanity's redemption must be seen in the greater context of the redemption of the entire cosmos. Humanity does not exist for its own sake. Humanity is called to glorify God by being the principal conduit through which God redeems and blesses the rest of creation. Paul spells this out in Romans 8.

> I consider that our present sufferings are not worth comparing with the glory that will be revealed in us. The creation waits in eager expectation for the sons of God to be revealed. For the creation was subjected to frustration, not by its own choice, but by the will of the one who subjected it, in hope that the creation itself will be liberated from its bondage to decay and brought into the glorious freedom of the children of God. We know that the whole creation has been groaning as in the pains of childbirth right up to the present time. Not only so, but we ourselves, who have the firstfruits of the Spirit, groan inwardly as we wait eagerly for our adoption as sons, the redemption of our bodies. (Rom 8:18–23)

In this passage, Paul explicitly draws a connection between the salvation of humanity and the salvation of creation: as believers are strengthened in their sufferings because of their hope in the resurrection, so creation "waits," knowing that it too will be liberated. In order to have a good understanding of this passage, it is imperative to know something about how the Old Testament looks forward to the restoration of the created order. An immediate consequence of the first couple's rebellion was disharmony within creation. We see this in God's censuring of Adam after he partook of the forbidden fruit.

> Cursed is the ground because of you; through painful toil you will eat of it all the days of your life. It will produce thorns and thistles for you, and you will eat the plants of the field. By the sweat of your brow you will eat your food until you return to the ground, since from it you were taken; for dust you are and to dust you will return. (Gen 3:17–19)

No doubt, as a consequence of the fall humanity was banished from the garden, "lest they eat from the tree of life and live forever"—forever, that

The Gospel and the Cross

is, in a fallen condition in which they live separate from God (Gen 3:22). But the initial statement of God to Adam concerns the disruption between humanity (the Hebrew "*adam*" variously refers both to the individual Adam and to humanity) and creation. Whereas up until that point Adam had tended the garden with peace, from then on his working of the ground would involve "painful toil" and the "sweat of his brow." Such disharmony was also felt between the animal kingdom and humanity, a point that is implied in God's statement to Noah following the flood:

> Be fruitful and increase in number and fill the earth. The fear and dread of you will fall upon all the beasts of the earth and all the birds of the air, upon every creature that moves along the ground, and upon all the fish of the sea; they are given into your hands. Everything that lives and moves will be food for you. Just as I gave you the green plants, I now give you everything. (Gen 9:1–3)

Presumably, then, whereas humanity was vegetarian prior to the fall in Genesis 3, in Noah's day a transition was made to a diet that included meat. But later prophets predicted that a time would come when there would be a return to the idyllic nature of the Garden in which perfect harmony abounded—harmony within the animal kingdom, harmony between animals and humanity, and harmony between all creation and God. In this regard Isaiah proclaimed the following:

> The wolf will live with the lamb, the leopard will lie down with the goat, the calf and the lion and the yearling together; and a little child will lead them. The cow will feed with the bear, their young will lie down together, and the lion will eat straw like the ox. The infant will play near the hole of the cobra, and the young child put his hand into the viper's nest. They will neither harm nor destroy on all my holy mountain, for the earth will be full of the knowledge of the Lord as the waters cover the sea. (Isa 11:6–9)

Romans 8 is a continuation of this concern to bring all existence back to an Edenic paradise. The ultimate concern of the New Testament is nothing less than the restoration of the perfect harmony that existed between God and creation in the beginning—in the words of Revelation, "a new heaven and a new earth" (Rev 21:1). The linchpin between the old age of sin and death, and the new age of righteousness and life, is the gospel of Christ—a key feature of which is the cross of Christ.

With its single-minded emphasis on the effects of the crucifixion of Christ for personal salvation, Evangelicalism as a whole has failed to understand that the cross of Christ equally has tremendous effects for all existence—the heavens, the earth, and the entire universe. No doubt, the effects of the crucifixion for individuals are great: the penalty for sin was canceled, the sinful are declared righteous, and salvation is open for all. But viewing the effects of the cross strictly in terms of individual salvation is to misunderstand the message of the cross.

The Cross and Suffering

The incarnation and the crucifixion need to be understood together, for both ends of the Jesus story inform us how God has chosen to redeem humanity. In both cases God chose what is homely and despised to bring redemption to the world—the manger in which baby Jesus lay was perhaps a damp and stench-filled cave that was used to house domesticated animals; and the cross from which "messianic pretender" Jesus hanged may simply have been a de-branched tree or crude timbers. Yet the power and presence of God resided in each: infant Jesus, the very temple of God; and crucified Jesus, through whom God was redeeming humanity. Jesus came into this world of suffering, and in suffering he left this world.

The given passage in Romans 8 similarly implies that the cross should be understood in light of suffering in general. So long as humanity lives on this side of eternity, suffering will exist—suffering from malnourishment and starvation, from overpopulation, from structural evil, from war, from poverty, from lack of education, from loneliness, from despair, from greed, from broken relationships, etc. Creation suffers with humanity—longing as it does to be restored even as the believer longs for the resurrection.

But the concern of the New Testament is not so much that of interpreting suffering in general in light of the cross, but interpreting persecution in light of the cross. Throughout the first centuries Christians were subjected to unrelenting persecution—particularly from Judaism (of which Christianity was originally a sect) and from the state. Jewish authorities persecuted Christians for allegedly subverting Moses, disrespecting the traditions of the fathers, and instigating violence from Rome. Roman authorities, in their turn, persecuted Christians for being atheists (Christians did not believe in the gods of the empire), for being treasonous (bowing before a Jewish peasant rather than bowing before the Emperor), and perhaps even for cannibalism ("eating the body and drinking the blood") and orgies (they had "love feasts," after all). In some respects Christians were treated

The Gospel and the Cross

as scapegoats, on whose heads all the troubles of society could be placed. In much of the early church, becoming a Christian was akin to signing one's own death certificate. The author of 2 Timothy could even say, "everyone who wants to live a godly life in Christ Jesus will be persecuted" (2 Tim 3:12).

Peter could similarly teach that Christians are not to understand persecution as something that is somehow contrary to following Jesus: "Dear friends, do not be surprised at the painful trial you are suffering, as though something strange were happening to you" (1 Pet 4:12). Peter was concerned to teach his readers that the story of Jesus must also be their story: "Christ suffered for you, leaving you an example, that you should follow in his steps" (1 Pet 2:21); "since Christ suffered in his body, arm yourselves also with the same attitude" (1 Pet 4:1). Luke also makes the same point in his treatment of the martyrdom of Stephen. While various Jewish authorities were stoning Stephen to death, Stephen prayed "Lord Jesus, receive my spirit" (Luke 7:59) and his last recorded words were "Lord, do not hold this sin against them" (Luke 7:60)—the former statement parallels Jesus's prayer "Father, into your hands I commit my spirit" (Luke 23:43), while the latter statement mirrors Jesus's petition for those who crucified him, "Father forgive them, for they don't know what they are doing" (Luke 23:34).

Not long ago I had the following conversation with an Evangelical minister (who I will refer to as "Bill").

John: I think that central to the Christian life is the ability to understand suffering in light of the sufferings of Jesus.

Bill: I can't agree, for the emphasis in the New Testament is that Jesus is victorious over suffering.

John: But the New Testament emphasis is not that Jesus is victorious *over* suffering but that Jesus is victorious *through* suffering. The two are very different.

Bill: Granted. But Jesus only suffered for one week at the end of his life, so suffering was not a huge part of his life, and focusing on it is to distort the gospel.

This is where the conversation ended, but perhaps the two of us will pick it up again where we left off. I do think that understanding (and embracing as our own) the suffering of Jesus is fundamental to the faith. The suffering of Jesus should also be understood as an outgrowth of the self-emptying of

God in Christ—for the divine humility involved in the incarnation is on the same trajectory as the suffering and crucifixion of Christ. What is presented to us in the New Testament is a seamless whole: the One who emptied himself for us, is the One who suffered on our behalf, is the One who was crucified for us. Jesus did all this for us, and following him involves going on the same journey toward death in order that we might know life. I loathe the teaching during holy week that says "It's Friday now, but Sunday's a com'n." Yes, the believer experiences victory over the cross, but only insofar as they first embrace the cross. On this side of eternity victory over the cross can only be known by living and experiencing the cross. The cross is, and must always be, central to Christian self-understanding.

I was once in a Roman Catholic church that had an empty cross (rather than a crucifix) on the sanctuary wall. A fellow Evangelical minister who was with me at the time stated that this was indicative of the great progression in Roman Catholic theology—for, according to this minister, the Roman Catholic church was beginning to understand that Jesus had triumphed over suffering, that he was no longer on the cross, and that atonement for sin had been made once and for all. In this minister's mind, the image of Jesus on the cross had no place in Christian theology. But from the perspective of the New Testament, the crucifixion of Christ is the model for Christian existence. The connection between the cross and Christian existence is explicitly made by Paul:

> I want to know Christ and the power of his resurrection and the fellowship of his sufferings by becoming like him in his death, if somehow I may attain the resurrection from the dead. (Phil 3:10–11)

Central to Paul's thought is "in Christ mysticism"—the believer abides in or is united with Jesus Christ. Consistent with this, Paul here equates knowing Christ with "the fellowship of his sufferings." This is a profound teaching. A favorite term in Evangelical circles is the Greek word *koinōnia*, which is typically translated as "fellowship." In addition to having fellowship with one another (1 John 1:7), believers have fellowship with the Father (1 John 1:3), the Son (1 Cor 1:9) and the Holy Spirit (2 Cor 13:14). But what is not commonly known is that Christians are equally called to have fellowship with the sufferings of Jesus. In the passage above, Paul contends that he wants to know "fellowship" with the sufferings of Christ. (It does not say, as the NIV reads, "the fellowship *of sharing in* his sufferings" but "the fellowship of his sufferings"). Paul similarly states that "the sufferings of Christ overflow into our lives" (2 Cor 1:5). In Philippians Paul could say, "It has been granted to you on behalf of Christ not only to believe on him, but also to suffer for him" (Phil 1:29). In Colossians we are told that Paul fills up in his flesh "what is still lacking in regard to Christ's afflictions" (Col 1:24). Peter similarly counseled his readers to rejoice, for they "are sharing Christ's sufferings" (1 Pet 4:13). Such teaching is contrary (even embarrassing) to Evangelical culture and thinking, which typically sees the suffering of Jesus as something that was done some two millennia ago—certainly not something in which ancient and modern believers alike are called to participate.

The Cross and Discipleship

Much of the gospel story is itself about the crucifixion of Jesus. The Gospel of Mark, which was likely the earliest Gospel, has nothing to say about Jesus's early years, and relatively little to say about Jesus's teachings, but it has much to say about the last week of Jesus's life. In Mark, it is as if Jesus was hurrying to the cross. Whether it was Jesus, Herod, a disciple or other characters in Mark who taught, acted, traveled, saw, or spoke—they did so "immediately." But during the trial of Jesus before Pilate and his subsequent crucifixion, "immediately" appears relatively infrequently. It is as if time had slowed down with the crucifixion. (While versions typically translate the Greek term *euthus* [pronounced "oo-thuss"], which appears dozens of times in Mark, as "immediately," they also translate it as "at once," "without delay," or "as soon as"—thereby obscuring Mark's emphasis on hastening to the cross.) But even as Mark speeds his readers to the crucifixion, he does not fail to emphasize that the cross does not simply concern eternal salvation, for it itself defines the nature of Christian existence. Mark underlines this point in his treatment of Peter's confession of Christ.

> Jesus went on with his disciples to the villages of Caesarea Philippi; and on the way he asked his disciples, "Who do people say that I am?" And they answered him, "John the Baptist; and others, Elijah; and still others, one of the prophets." He asked them, "But who do you say that I am?" Peter answered him, "You are the Messiah." And he sternly ordered them not to tell anyone about him. Then he began to teach them that the Son of Man must undergo great suffering, and be rejected by the elders, the chief priests, and the scribes, and be killed, and after three days rise again. He said all this quite openly. And Peter took him aside and began to rebuke him. But turning and looking at his disciples, he rebuked Peter and

> said, "Get behind me, Satan! For you are setting your mind not on divine things but on human things." He called the crowd with his disciples, and said to them, "If any want to become my followers, let them deny themselves and take up their cross and follow me. For those who want to save their life will lose it, and those who lose their life for my sake, and for the sake of the gospel, will save it. For what will it profit them to gain the whole world and forfeit their life? Indeed, what can they give in return for their life? Those who are ashamed of me and of my words in this adulterous and sinful generation, of them the Son of Man will also be ashamed when he comes in the glory of his Father with the holy angels." (Mark 8:27–38)

On the surface of things, Peter's famous declaration that Jesus is "the Christ" was on the mark. Yet Peter's understanding of what it meant to be "the Christ" was fundamentally flawed, for Jesus did not come to be victorious over the hated Roman oppressors, but to suffer greatly, and to be rejected and killed prior to rising from the dead. Important for our purposes, Jesus rebuked Peter for failing to see that the Christ would suffer greatly, and he used the opportunity to teach that all who follow him must, like him, take up their cross. Jesus's rebuke of Peter is very harsh. In addition to implying that Satan was speaking through Peter, Jesus told Peter that failing to believe that the Son of Man would suffer is to set one's mind on human rather than divine concerns. Jesus then told both the crowd and his disciples that carrying one's cross is integral to being a follower of him. Contrary to common understanding, bearing the cross is not a matter of patiently putting up with various difficulties in life—like unemployment, divorce, or cancer. Taking up one's cross, rather, is all about living for Jesus irrespective of the consequences. The Christian is called to pay no regard for the applause of this world, and, like Jesus, to live only for God—even if doing so involves literal martyrdom. Those who bear the cross deny self-interest, and they lose their lives for Jesus's sake—for they know that living to gain the world is to forfeit one's life. Peter evidently took Jesus's rebuke to heart, for, like the Gospel of Mark, 1 Peter emphasizes that Christians will suffer for their faith: "For to this you have been called, because Christ also suffered for you, leaving you an example, so that you should follow in his steps" (1 Pet 2:21).

An example from Paul's writings that concerns the relationship between the cross and discipleship is found at the close of Galatians 2.

> I have been crucified with Christ; and it is no longer I who live, but it is Christ who lives in me. And the life I now live in the flesh

> I live by faith in the Son of God, who loved me and gave himself
> for me. (Gal 2:19–20)

Paul here pronounces his self-understanding with reference to the crucifixion of Christ. Paul asserts that he himself has been crucified with Christ, such that he no longer lives but Christ lives within him. Such death to self brought life, for Christ himself then indwelt Paul. This truth produced in Paul great fortitude, for it enabled him to withstand tremendous persecution. Paul could similarly state elsewhere that "we always carry around in our body the death of Jesus, so that the life of Jesus may also be revealed in our body" (2 Cor 4:10).

The Cross and Wisdom

In the preceding section I noted that the way of the cross is the way of Christian discipleship. This is altogether counter-intuitive in the Western world, for we assume that success comes through hard work and individual actualization. Yet the idea that the cross is God's means of bringing redemption to humanity is as counter-cultural as it is counter-intuitive, for many of the values of Western society are the very inverse of the message of the cross. The scandal of the cross equally confronted the values of first-century society. Paul discusses the scandal of the cross to his society in the following passage:

> For the message of the cross is foolishness to those who are perishing, but to us who are being saved it is the power of God. . . . Jews demand miraculous signs and Greeks look for wisdom, but we preach Christ crucified: a stumbling block to Jews and foolishness to Gentiles, but to those whom God has called, both Jews and Greeks, Christ the power of God and the wisdom of God. (1 Cor 1:18, 22–24)

The message of the cross was offensive to Judaism, for a crucified messiah was a contradiction in terms. Rather than dying on a cross, the messiah was to lead the nation in miraculous victory over its gentile oppressors. The message of the cross was likewise foolish to the Greeks—for whereas Greek philosophy is the product of sophisticated reasoning, the message of the cross is physical and homely. Yet in such "foolishness" is found the very wisdom of God. Paul's counsel to the Corinthians was that they were to find their grounding in the cross rather than clever thinking.

There are many examples in church history where one church or another has sought to make the message of the cross more palatable to its world. Perhaps this has partly been due to the attempt to enculturate the gospel. More often than not, however, one church or another has unreflectively syncretized the message of the cross to the *Zeitgeist* of the world—such that the proclamation of the given church became indistinguishable from the values of its society. History abounds with examples. In the twentieth century one can think of the marriage between German Christians and the message of their Führer, covenant theology and apartheid policies in South Africa, the slogan "God bless America" even while the nation's foreign policies have been rife with exploitation, and the unreflective acceptance of Canadian mainline churches of the government's residential school solution to "the aboriginal problem." In all such cases churches have sought to legitimize their understanding of the gospel to their society by embracing the values of the society itself. Far from being a light to the world, churches have unwittingly become indistinguishable from their world. Evangelicalism has, in some ways, followed suit. Not unlike Evangelicalism's assimilation of Enlightenment categories of thought, it has also tended to embrace Western values even as it has sought to be faithful to its understanding of the gospel.

With regard to societal influence, I can think of three reasons for Evangelicalism's failure to understand the cross. To begin with, Western society has no room for the message of the cross. Suffering is contrary to progress. Suffering undermines hard work. Suffering stifles potential. Suffering has great economic consequences. Those who suffer experience shame. Those who suffer are hid from society behind bars, in psychiatric hospitals, in slums, and in hospices. The litany of complaints against suffering is very long. Altogether confusing, then, is the notion that the message of the cross is somehow integral to Christian faith. I am reminded of a friend who wished to buy a necklace with a crucifix. My friend went to a jewelery store, and after the jeweler showed her the necklaces with crosses, the jeweler said, "We also have some crosses with a little man on them." If suffering does not sit well in the Western mind, altogether unfathomable is the notion that the suffering of "a little man" on a cross is somehow an example for us to follow. Given that Evangelicalism is a child of Western society, it may not surprise us that the cross does not find an easy place in the Evangelical mind.

The Gospel and the Cross

A second reason for Evangelicalism's failure to understand the cross concerns its emphasis on progress—which is perhaps suggestive of its marriage to capitalistic concerns. Evangelicalism often seems to be little more than the spiritualization of the Western economic ethos. In the Evangelical mind, a sure sign of God's approval is growth, size, and influence—number of members in the "megachurch"; number of members whose giving exceeds the 10 percent tithe; and number of programs, committees, and cell groups. The blessing of God is proportionate to the progress or growth of such figures from one year to the next. Perhaps the most frightening parallel between capitalism and Evangelicalism is their self-interest. Capitalism succeeds primarily because people are greedy, even as Evangelicalism's gospel is often marred by "what's in it for me?" thinking, or presenting God as the infinite therapist who is "just" longing to help us through "inner healing" in all our marital, parental, and financial hardships. Here we have "Christianity lite" in all its glory. Such self-interest is most pronounced in the capitalistic concern with privatization. Even as governments seek to privatize such things as health care, transportation, and education with greater prosperity in mind, so Evangelicalism seeks to privatize the gospel: the concern is not the greater community, but how "Jesus, who is my *personal* Lord and Savior" can help me prosper in this life and eventually get me to heaven. But Jesus is not, properly speaking, *your personal* Lord. He is *the* Lord of the universe!

A final reason (with some lovely exceptions) that Evangelicalism has failed to understand the cross concerns the triumphalism that it exhibits. A church that I used to attend began every service with the hymn "Victory in Jesus." While the words to this hymn may well be innocent enough, with hindsight it seems to me that for this community "victory" included success in business, in relationships, in parenting, in politics, and in health. Yes, there is every reason to be triumphant. Demonic forces have been vanquished. The kingdom is a present reality. The church will prevail over all that threatens it. Nothing can thwart the sure promises of God. While none of these declarations are contrary to what the New Testament teaches, they are only true to the Bible when they are seen together with their opposites. Yes, demonic forces have been defeated, but only insofar as they are retreating, for their power still lurks. Yes, the Kingdom of God is a present reality, but it exists alongside the kingdom of darkness. Yes, the church will prevail, but only through many setbacks. Yes, the promises of God are sure, but their fulfilment will likely come in a most surprising way.

Born Again and Beyond

Because Western Evangelicalism has wed itself to the Western *Zeitgeist*, its comprehension of Christian faith has been polluted. In the preceding paragraphs I limited the discussion to various aspects of the Western ethos that distort the message of the cross. Much more could be said along these lines, for the commonalities between Western values and Evangelicalism are many. One could equally address the parallels shared by Western consumerism, militarism, imperialism, and its spiritual counterparts in Western Evangelicalism—be they "name it and claim it" teaching, "spiritual warfare" emphases, or "assuming authority in the name of Jesus." Because it has unreflectively mixed the Western ethos with Christian faith, Evangelicalism's message of the gospel and the cross has often been all but compromised.

Chapter Five

Salvation and Spirituality

NOT UNLIKE ITS FAILURE to reflect on *knowing* in an adequate fashion, Evangelicalism has done a poor job in addressing *being*. Given that the three members of the triad are interconnected and that they share a symbiotic relationship, Evangelicalism's oversight in this regard has also been detrimental to its emphasis on *doing*. In Christian terms, ortho-being expresses itself in particular in the field of spirituality. The subject of spirituality in Evangelicalism is hardly present. While there are lovely exceptions—such as several books written by Richard J. Foster, Philip Yancey, and some others, they are exactly that, exceptions. The contents of such works are largely dependent upon spiritual classics from Western or Eastern Christian traditions. This is not to slight Foster or Yancey in the slightest. Quite the contrary, I applaud them, for the spiritual wisdom found in the Roman Catholic and Orthodox traditions far surpasses, both in depth and breadth, what Protestantism has produced. Given the high regard that Evangelicalism expresses for Scripture, its relative silence on the subject of spirituality is somewhat bewildering, for the Scriptures are themselves chock-full of teachings regarding being—purity of heart, forgiveness, obedience, love, the fruits of the Spirit, etc.

SPIRITUALITY AND CONVERSION

One reason why Evangelicalism as a whole has failed to emphasize the subject of spirituality comes out of its insistence that conversion is an event rather than a process. A highly regarded component of Evangelical services is the place given for "testimonies." While I delight in hearing how God has worked in people's lives to bring them out of darkness into light, and despair into hope, I nevertheless often come away with a feeling of incompleteness—as if I had read only the opening chapter of an exciting book only to lose the book. I also want to delight in the way in which God continues to work in the person's life, for this is equally exciting. Yet all too often testimonies stop short of telling the whole story. "Happily ever after" must never be assumed on this side of eternity: the One who began a good work in you is the very One who will bring this work to completion, but only when Christ returns (Phil 1:6). But if Evangelicalism is correct in its insistence that conversion is an event in which all one's sins have been washed away, little room is left for growth in the spiritual life.

Years ago I attended a charismatic conference. To my dismay and bewilderment, behind me sat two nuns robed in their habits. I thought that prior to attending such a conference people really ought to be saved. With evangelistic fervor I asked the sisters, "Have you been born again?" One of them replied with confidence, "We are born again every day." This reply ended the conversation, for it was altogether bewildering to me. I was prepared, with Bible in hand, to take them down the "Romans road to salvation" and to show them from the Bible that works could not save them. They simply were not playing by the rules, for they introduced a thought that was completely alien to my understanding of salvation. At an exegetical level there can be little doubt that "born again" of John 3 refers to a one-time event, but at a more general level seeds of doubt had been planted in my own mind. I now smile at a more recent conversation that I had with a Baptist minister. Thinking that I was on his side—a theological good guy—the minister smugly said, "I believe that some Roman Catholics are Christians." With little hesitation I replied, "I likewise believe that some Baptists are Christians." The expression the minister then gave me was probably like the one that I had given to the nuns years earlier.

Over the years I became increasingly aware, largely for biblical reasons, that the Evangelical emphasis on salvation as an event is problematic. While there are many passages in the New Testament that use the past tense of the Greek verb *sōzō* (pronounced "sew-zew") with reference to eternal salvation, there are others that use the present tense ("are being saved") as well as the future tense ("will be saved"). Here are examples of the present tense:

> For the message of the cross is foolishness to those who are perishing, but to us who *are being saved* it is the power of God. (1 Cor 1:18)
>
> For we are to God the aroma of Christ among those who *are being saved* and those who are perishing. (2 Cor 2:15)

Here is one example of the future tense:

> This is a sign to them that they will be destroyed, but that you *will be saved*—and that by God. (Phil 1:28)

Here is an example where past, present, and future are united:

> Since we *have now been justified* by his blood, how much more *shall we be saved* from God's wrath through him! For if, when we were God's enemies, *we were reconciled* to him through the death of his Son, how much more, *having been reconciled, shall we be saved* through his life! (Rom 5:9–10)

Far from simply an event in the past, salvation involves the past, the present, and the future.

It is the present tense ("are being saved") that is of particular importance to the field of spirituality: the Christian longs to grow in love for God and people, to be the instrument of Jesus to the poor and lonely, to excel in the fruits of the Spirit—none of which is easy. As John Bunyan assumes throughout *Pilgrim's Progress*, the road to the celestial city is fraught with perils—Vanity Fair, the Slough of Despondency, Doubting Castle, and the like. While "Christian" leaves his weight of sin early on in the allegory, his salvation is not fully realized until he comes to the celestial city. This is all delightfully consistent with Paul's words to the Philippians:

> Continue to work out your salvation with fear and trembling. (Phil 2:12)

Such words need to be understood in their context. Preceding this verse is the celebrated *kenōsis* (pronounced "ke-know-sis," which means "self-emptying") hymn of Philippians 2:6–11.

> Who, being in very nature God,
> did not consider equality with God something to be grasped,
> but made himself nothing,
> taking the very nature of a servant,
> being made in human likeness.

> And being found in appearance as a man,
> he humbled himself
> and became obedient to death—
> even death on a cross!
> Therefore God exalted him to the highest place
> and gave him the name that is above every name,
> that at the name of Jesus every knee should bow,
> in heaven and on earth and under the earth,
> and every tongue confess that Jesus Christ is Lord,
> to the glory of God the Father.

Throughout the centuries this hymn has received much attention. Many suggest that the hymn predates Paul's ministry for it includes language and themes that are not present elsewhere in Paul's writings. If indeed this is the case, we see that shortly after the Christ event (perhaps even in the 40s of the first century), some Christians already had a very advanced understanding of the nature of Jesus—who was "in the form of God" and "in the form of a servant" all at once, and who shares God's name.[1] But Paul did not include this hymn to make a theological statement as such. Paul's concern, rather, was pastoral insofar as he here invited the Philippians to imitate Jesus. He included the hymn to illustrate how the Philippians should be humble toward one another. The verses that precede the hymn make this clear:

> If you have any encouragement from being united with Christ, if any comfort from his love, if any fellowship with the Spirit, if any tenderness and compassion, then make my joy complete by being like-minded, having the same love, being one in spirit and purpose. Do nothing out of selfish ambition or vain conceit, but in humility consider others better than yourselves. Each of you should look not only to your own interests, but also to the interests of others. Your attitude should be the same as that of Christ Jesus. (Phil 2:1–6a)

It is after these verses in which Paul urges the Philippians to be humble that he includes the *kenōsis* hymn. Following the hymn Paul states, "continue to work out your salvation with fear and trembling" (Phil 2:12). Working out

---

1. "Every knee shall bow . . . and every tongue confess" is a citation of Isaiah 45:23, in which Yahweh is speaking with reference to how universal humanity will prostrate themselves before him. The fact that early Christians quoted passages from the Old Testament that referred to Yahweh and applied them to Jesus (as here) indicates that, from their perspective, Jesus was one with Yahweh (see also the use of Ps 68:18 in Eph 4:8–10).

Salvation and Spirituality

one's salvation is all about growing in humility, dying to self, and striving to be like Jesus. The nun was altogether correct: "We are born again every day." Salvation is not simply an event. It may well begin as an event, but on this side of eternity the event never ceases. The Spirit of God is forever encouraging us to become imitators of Jesus—at times forbidding us to accept the status quo, at times disciplining us through a dark night of the soul, and at all times wanting us to grow in hope.

SPIRITUALITY AND HOPE

As I noted above, the New Testament refers to salvation as something that takes place in the past, the present, and the future. Salvation covers the time from original confession to resurrection. But even this movement from past to present to future is not the whole story, for the process of salvation started not with our repentance, but with God's grace:

> For he chose us in him before the creation of the world to be holy and blameless in his sight. (Eph 1:4)

> We love because he first loved us. (1 John 4:19)

Just as God in his kindness brought us to salvation and keeps us in salvation, so God in his mercy prepared the circumstances for our coming to faith in the first place. Knowledge of this fact produces hope in the believer.

The New Testament's use of the term *hope* has no correspondence with the way that this term is typically understood in the modern world. You might say "I hope that you win the lottery" or "I hope that she enjoyed the movie." But when Paul refers to the "hope of salvation" he means something altogether different. In the former case there is great uncertainty—someone else will likely win the lottery, and given that she has little regard for movies, it is doubtful that she enjoyed this one. Additionally, in the former instances such hope will not have any effect on the way you presently live your life. In contrast with this, hope in the New Testament concerns the way in which the promised future shapes the present. It is hope that enables us to transfer the qualities of heaven to our lives in the here and now.

One of the more significant aspects of Evangelical theology that needs an overhaul is its theology of hope. Hope is implicit in Jesus's prayer "your kingdom come, your will be done on earth as it is in heaven." Living in the kingdom on this earth is to be a reflection of the kingdom in heaven. Jesus's will for humanity was that as it embraced the values of the kingdom of God, the kingdom would flourish on this broken earth. Even while we await the full realization of the kingdom, we are called to live in this world as though we were living in heaven. Imagine for a moment what heaven will be like: perfect peace, full acceptance, everlasting love, and unfettered joy. Now let us take these qualities and embody them in our own lives.

Such was the significance of "hope" for Paul that he consistently mentioned it together with "faith" and "love."

> And now these three remain: *faith*, *hope* and *love*. But the greatest of these is love. (1 Cor 13:13)

> We have heard of your *faith* in Christ Jesus and of the *love* you have for all the saints—the *faith* and *love* that spring from the *hope* that is stored up for you in heaven and that you have already heard about in the word of truth, the gospel. (Col 1:4–5)

> We continually remember before our God and Father your work produced by *faith*, your labor prompted by *love*, and your endurance inspired by *hope* in our Lord Jesus Christ. (1 Thess 1:3)

> But since we belong to the day, let us be self-controlled, putting on *faith* and *love* as a breastplate, and the *hope* of salvation as a helmet. (1 Thess 5:8)

For Paul, the three virtues of faith, hope, and love are integral to the process of salvation. I think that we probably have a good idea about the general meanings of faith and love. But it seems to me that we may not have such a good understanding of the meaning of hope. Paul's conviction that knowledge of the promised future should shape present Christian life accords with other passages in the New Testament. The author of Titus, for example, could state that "the knowledge of the truth that leads to godliness" is a "knowledge resting on the *hope* of eternal life, which God, who does not lie, promised before the beginning of time" (Titus 1:1–2). This discussion of hope in the New Testament is of great spiritual import, for it impacts the way that we love God with our this-worldly selves. How I wish that those who devote so much time, energy, and financial resources to publishing books about the end of the world would redirect only a fraction of their efforts to discussing how knowing how the world will all end ought to shape our present lives. This is what hope is all about.

Salvation and Spirituality

While I was a young Baptist minister on Vancouver Island I spent untold hours studying, debating, and teaching various end-times matters. I deceived myself into thinking that doing so must be a sign of my spiritual vitality. But as I look back, I see that trying to understand the future did not help me to live a better Christian life. I had relatively little time for such practicalities. There was doctrinal work that needed doing. Yet I was not altogether duped by myself, for I remember receiving a booklet in the mail called "88 Reasons Why the Lord Will Return in 1988." While I said to myself, "What a silly waste of time," I did not for a moment think that I too might have been approaching the whole subject from the wrong angle. When we look at those passages in the New Testament that concern the end of the world, we see that without exception the authors' concern was not to call his readers to speculate about the end, but to be transformed by the knowledge that the end was at hand. In defense of this, in the following paragraphs I will limit the discussion to Revelation's emphasis on remaining true to Jesus in the face of opposition and persecution. In this regard, Revelation often uses the Greek noun *hupomonē* (pronounced "who-paw-maw-nay"), which the NIV translates as "patient endurance."

> I, John, your brother and companion in the suffering and kingdom and *patient endurance* that are ours in Jesus, was on the island of Patmos because of the word of God and the testimony of Jesus. (Rev 1:9)

> If anyone is to go into captivity, into captivity they will go. If anyone is to be killed with the sword, with the sword they will be killed. This calls for *patient endurance* and faithfulness on the part of God's people. (Rev 13:10)

Similar terminology is behind Jesus's counsel to the seven churches to remain faithful in spite of their present circumstances:

> Do not be afraid of what you are about to suffer. I tell you, the devil will put some of you in prison to test you, and you will suffer persecution for ten days. *Be faithful*, even to the point of death, and I will give you life as your victor's crown. (Rev 2:10)

> I know that you have little strength, yet you have kept my word and have not denied my name. . . . Since you have kept my command to *endure patiently*, I will also keep you from the hour of trial that is going to come on the whole world to test the inhabitants of the earth. (Rev 3:8–10)

Believers could patiently endure because they knew that God brings nations and kings into existence, and it is God who brings them to naught. It is God who will send the Lamb, the Word of God, in great glory to judge the world in righteousness and to set up an eternal kingdom on earth. Knowing that all this is so, believers would be better able to endure hardship. John teaches elsewhere that the anticipation of Christ's return similarly enables the believer to grow in purity:

> We know that when he appears we shall be like him for we shall see him as he is. Everyone who has this hope in him purifies himself, just as he is pure. (1 John 3:2–3)

While the teaching that one's understanding of the future should shape the present is fundamental to most "end-times" passages, it needs to be stressed that the future does not simply shape how the present is understood; rather, the future is itself experienced in the present.

> I tell you the truth, *a time is coming and has now come* when the dead will hear the voice of the Son of God and those who hear will live. (John 5:25)

> Jesus said to her, "I am the resurrection and the life. The one who believes in me will live, even though they die; and whoever lives and believes in me will never die. (John 11:25–26)

In both examples we see that Jesus unites the present and the future: while the physically dead will be resurrected on the last day, the spiritually dead can experience resurrection right now. Similarly, while much of Revelation is concerned with the future apocalypse and the renewal of all things, at precisely the same time Revelation assumes that such eventualities are already known in the present. This is what Christian hope is all about; and this tends to be contrary to Evangelicalism's approach.

Up to this point in my treatment of the subject of hope I assume that I have not ruffled many feathers. But I expect that what I am about to say—even though it is solidly consistent both with the New Testament and with what the church has always taught—will be more seriously questioned. In the following paragraphs I will contend that the subject of hope in the New Testament is tied to belief that the afterlife will involve living on a physical earth, and that gospel hope in this life therefore necessarily includes physical matters—feeding the poor, defending human rights, engaging in politics, and caring for the environment.

Salvation and Spirituality

Let us first consider the contention that the afterlife will involve living on a physical earth. The popular belief that eternity will involve living as a disembodied soul with other souls in a spiritual place called heaven is, quite frankly, both non-biblical and worldly in the extreme. Yes, heaven exists. Yes, the Bible teaches that believers will go to heaven when they die. But from the perspective of the New Testament, heaven will only be the place that believers go to prior to the second coming of Jesus—at which time the bodily resurrection of the dead will take place (including those in heaven) and eternity will be spent in new bodies on a physical world. Heaven, then, may be likened to a blissful holding tank, an interim resting place for the faithful who have died prior to the return of Jesus. While this teaching may sound rather dubious to some, let it be known that this has *always* been the teaching of the church—right from its inception in the early first century. This is not even disputable. (Any credible book concerning Christian theology, however conservative or liberal it might be, will make this point. You might here pause to take another look at 1 Corinthians 15.)

In most instances in which someone in the Book of Acts preaches the gospel, resurrection, not heaven, is part of the message. Similarly, "hope" is tied to the resurrection rather than heaven.

> Then Paul . . . called out in the Sanhedrin, "My brothers, I am a Pharisee, the son of a Pharisee. I stand on trial because of my *hope* in the *resurrection* of the dead." (Acts 23:6)

> I have the same *hope* in God as these men, that there will be a *resurrection* of both the righteous and the wicked. (Acts 24:15)

The popular teaching that heaven, not the resurrection, is the ultimate hope is consistent with Greek thinking. In the ancient Greek world ultimate reality was limited to spiritual existence—whether it be the "forms" of Plato, the "fullness" of Gnosticism, the "spirit" in Manichaeism, or various teachings at the popular level. Material existence was, at best, a divine afterthought or accident. Salvation often consisted of deliverance from the material order. In some Christian circles such pro-spirit thinking became manifest in various sectarian groups, as with Docetism—the teaching that the Christ only "seemed" to have a body. In a more general way such thinking sometimes led to libertinism—which taught that because the flesh is of no concern, what one does in the flesh is of no consequence. The early church regarded all such teaching as being contrary to the gospel—more specifically, to the doctrines of the incarnation and the resurrection. If, the party of the Pharisees reasoned, God created a perfect physical world, it follows that he will restore the physical world to perfection—contending otherwise is to say that God made a mistake in creating the physical world in the first place. The early church similarly reasoned that if God (who is Spirit) became a human (who is physical), it follows that physical reality must be celebrated along with spiritual reality. Any teaching that somehow undermines the created world was therefore regarded as being contrary to Christian faith.

While much of the New Testament challenges Greek thinking regarding material existence, one of the greatest affronts to such thinking is John's declaration that "the Word became flesh" (John 1:14). In the Greek mind, such a statement was self-contradictory. The pure Word (which governed the entire cosmos) could no more assume flesh than fire could become water. The two categories were mutually exclusive—both in terms of existence (physical reality and spiritual reality) and in terms of quality of existence (corrupted reality and pure reality). Yes, the Word was in the beginning. Yes, it was through the Word that all things were created. Yes, there was life to be found in the Word. But to say that "the Word became flesh" is altogether outside of Greek thinking.

In spite of its insistence on the incarnation of God in Jesus—and with it, the acknowledgment that the created world is good—throughout the centuries Greek-like thinking has proven to be more attractive than what the Bible teaches. Such thinking is presupposed in much of medieval monasticism, segments of which have regarded hatred of all things physical as somehow being virtuous. Disregard for all things physical raised its head in kill-joy Puritanism in seventeenth-century New England. An argument has also been made that Greek-like thinking was presupposed in various Pietistic movements in the seventeenth and eighteenth centuries. Such attitudes toward all things physical are similarly seen in Evangelicalism's emphasis that salvation is strictly a spiritual affair. As with its adoption of Enlightenment thinking, Evangelicalism has also unwittingly bought into a worldview that tends to disparage the physical world. The way in which a Greek-like mindset impinges on how the Christian life is lived is what troubles me most of all. Through much of the twentieth century there was a controversy regarding the "Social Gospel" (as opposed to the "Salvation Gospel") within North American Evangelicalism. The very existence of such a controversy is, in my mind, telltale of Evangelicalism's failure to be incarnational in this world, for any gospel that is not at the same time social

Salvation and Spirituality

is no gospel at all—to love God is to love one's neighbor. Wishing to love God without at the same time striving to love one's neighbor is simply impossible. Theologically speaking, failing to love one's neighbor may amount to a failure to understand what the necessary implications of the doctrines of the incarnation and resurrection are—namely, being Christ's hands and feet in this real and physical world. This is God's good world. Fleeing from the needs of the world is to flee from God.

What of "environmental" initiatives? Is caring for the earth somehow contrary to Christian faith? Does concern for the environment lead one away from the gospel, perhaps down a slippery slope toward the worship of "Mother Earth"? Whether climate change is due to a planetary cycle, or whether it is due to the selfish use of fossil fuels is beside the point. The simple fact is that billions of poor people through the world are suffering from climate change: oceans rise and people on coastal lands lose their lands; with the melting of glaciers, rivers bearing fresh water dry up; and as global temperatures rise desertification of arable land increases. While pockets of the Evangelical world are addressing such issues, Evangelicalism as a whole seems to have little to say. "Famines, droughts, and pestilences are, after all, signs of the end of the world. Let the physical world perish. What really matters is the salvation of souls." I doubt that the world's poor have this view, for such thinking can only come from those whose finances, livelihoods, homes, and family members are not immediately affected by the environmental crisis—"whatever you did not do for one of the least of these, you did not do for me" (Matt 25:45).

Believing that Christ will return, that the dead will be raised, and that this physical world will be restored together with the cosmos, are instruments of hope. The follower of Jesus uses such truths to bring hope where there is despair, and to grow in love for God and others even when darkness reigns.

SPIRITUALITY AND LOVE

Shortly after returning from Nigeria I had a conversation with my friend Richard. At the time I was feeling very down. I asked him, "Do you think that we can be obedient to God without first loving Jesus?" Richard did not quite know how to answer this question. Knowing that Richard was committed to being obedient to God, I then asked him, "Do you love Jesus?" Richard's answer was "Yeah, I guess that I do." I could not say as much at the time. Yes, I believed that Jesus died for me. Yes, I believed in his kingdom, and that he would eventually return. But I could not *with integrity* say that I loved Jesus. Evangelicalism has similarly been noticeably silent over what it means to love God with all one's heart. No, loving God with one's heart is not referring to faithfulness to Scripture, to obedience, to evangelism, to defending the rights of the unborn, or even to embodying the fruits of the Spirit. While love for God may certainly work itself out in these ways, such activities are not to be equated with love for God. I readily agree that the Western world typically has a fractured understanding of love—an understanding that often confuses love with infatuation, lust, self-interest, and fleeting emotions. But this in no way undermines the fact that love does include emotion. When the Scriptures invite us to love God with our hearts, with everything that we are, this surely includes our emotions.

Perhaps this is why the Song of Songs is in the Scriptures. While it originally concerned love shared between a man and a woman, both early Judaism and early Christianity interpreted the Song of Songs as respectively concerning God's love for Israel or the church. (Up until late medieval times, the Song of Songs received more attention by biblical commentators than any other book in the Bible—the only exception being the Gospel of John.) We can of course debate this traditional interpretation, but this is not the issue at hand. The very fact that our forebears interpreted the Song of Songs in this way underlines the point that they believed that God is to be enjoyed, cherished, and embraced—in one word, loved. The subject of spirituality addresses just this. And if we are truly interested in right-*knowing* and right-*doing*, we must likewise be interested, even consumed, by the subject of right-*being*, which, for the Christian, is inextricably tied to love for God.

Bernard of Clairvaux addressed the subject of love for God in a delightful manner. Bernard contended that there are four degrees of love through which the pilgrim journeys. The first degree of love is "love of self for self's sake." At this stage the individual is only concerned with self: satisfaction of physical appetites, love of vainglory, un-relinquished pride, and living only to enhance ego. The second degree of love is "love of God for self's sake." At this stage the individual loves God with a catch—God will rescue from hell the one who believes in and serves him. The third stage is "love of God for God's sake." From Bernard's perspective, it is possible for people to live on this level on a regular basis—even though the tendency might be to fight continuously against returning to stage two. The fourth stage is "love of self for God's sake." At this stage the soul of the individual enjoys mystical unity with the Spirit of God. As fired steel seems to become indistinct from the fire that envelops it, so the soul becomes one with God. Bernard suggests that this stage is not even experienced in heaven, but only after the resurrection—for so long as the body and the soul are not united there cannot be perfect bliss (see Rom 8:23). While Bernard's understanding of the four stages of love is perhaps the best known, it bears mentioning that for almost two millennia now much of the Christian spiritual tradition has been concerned with the subjects of love for God and love for people. Whether it was from the desert fathers, a towering mystic like Theresa of Avila, St. John of the Cross, or "the little flower" of Lisieux, no one subject has pervaded spiritual literature as has love for God. Such writings have in common the teaching that the necessary corollary of love for God is love for people—a teaching that is, of course, central to the New Testament itself. The author of 1 John is most forthright on this point:

> If anyone says, "I love God," yet hates his brother or sister, he is a liar. For anyone who does not love his brother or sister, whom he has seen, cannot love God, whom he has not seen. And he has given us this command: Whoever loves God must also love his brother or sister. (1 John 4:20–21)

Closely tied to the teaching that whoever loves God must also love their neighbor is the teaching that service to others is inseparable from service to Jesus. In the Parable of the Sheep and Goats both the righteous and the wicked were surprised to learn that the way they served (or failed to serve) others is the way they served (or failed to serve) Jesus himself:

> When the Son of Man comes in his glory, and all the angels with him, he will sit on his throne in heavenly glory. All the nations will be gathered before him, and he will separate the people one from another as a shepherd separates the sheep from the goats. He will put the sheep on his right and the goats on his left. Then the King will say to those on his right, "Come, you who are blessed by my Father; take your inheritance, the kingdom prepared for you since the creation of the world. For I was hungry and you gave me something to eat, I was thirsty and you gave me something to drink, I was a stranger and you invited me in, I needed clothes and you clothed me, I was sick and you looked after me, I was in prison and you came to visit me." Then the righteous will answer him, "Lord, when did we see you hungry and feed you, or thirsty and give you something to drink? When did we see you a stranger and invite you in, or needing clothes and clothe you? When did

we see you sick or in prison and go to visit you?" The King will reply, "I tell you the truth, *whatever you did for one of the least of these brothers of mine, you did for me.*" Then he will say to those on his left, "Depart from me, you who are cursed, into the eternal fire prepared for the devil and his angels. For I was hungry and you gave me nothing to eat, I was thirsty and you gave me nothing to drink, I was a stranger and you did not invite me in, I needed clothes and you did not clothe me, I was sick and in prison and you did not look after me." They also will answer, "Lord, when did we see you hungry or thirsty or a stranger or needing clothes or sick or in prison, and did not help you?" He will reply, "I tell you the truth, *whatever you did not do for one of the least of these, you did not do for me.*" Then they will go away to eternal punishment, but the righteous to eternal life. (Matt 25:31–46)

Similar to the Parable of the Sheep and Goats, when Jesus encountered Saul on the road to Damascus, Jesus referred to himself as the one whom Saul was persecuting—even though it was the church that Saul persecuted:

> He fell to the ground and heard a voice say to him, "Saul, Saul, why do you persecute me?" "Who are you, Lord?" Saul asked. "I am Jesus, whom you are persecuting," he replied. (Acts 9:4–5)

Paul's favorite metaphor for the church is the "body of Christ." In this line of thinking, mistreatment of any member of the body therefore amounts to mistreatment of Christ himself:

> When you sin against your brothers and sisters in this way and wound their weak conscience, you sin against Christ. (1 Cor 8:12)

The New Testament teaching that love for God is necessarily expressed in love for people is simply beautiful. In more recent times one can see how the ministry of Mother Theresa of Calcutta was shaped by the thinking of St. Therese of Lisieux: the simple and even homely things through which St. Therese adored Jesus became the poor and homeless people through whom Mother Theresa adored Jesus. Below the crucifix on a wall of Mother Theresa's Calcutta mission are the words "I thirst." Mother Theresa interpreted such words of Jesus on the cross as ultimately referring to the way in which Jesus suffers with the poor. Mother Theresa's mission was to alleviate such thirst. Mother Theresa's contention that loving the poor is to love Jesus is captured in a beautiful manner in a prayer that she penned for the Sisters of Charity:

> Dearest Lord, may I see you today and every day in the person of your sick, and, while nursing them, minister to you. Though you hide yourself behind the unattractive disguise of the irritable, the exacting, the unreasonable, may I still recognize you, and say: "Jesus, my patient, how sweet it is to serve you." Lord, give me this seeing faith, then my work will never be monotonous. I will ever find joy in humouring the fancies and gratifying the wishes of all poor sufferers. O beloved sick, how doubly dear you are to me when you personify Christ; and what a privilege is mine to be allowed to tend you. Sweetest Lord, make me appreciative of the dignity of my high vocation, and its many responsibilities. Never permit me to disgrace it by giving way to coldness, unkindness, or impatience. And O God, while you are Jesus my patient, deign also to be to me a patient Jesus, bearing with my faults, looking only to my intention, which is to love and serve you in the person of each one of your sick. Lord, increase my faith, bless my efforts and work, now and for evermore, Amen.[2]

This prayer unites love for God with love for people. Consistent with Mother Theresa's message that everyone bears the image of God, she prayed that she would be able to see Jesus in the most destitute of people—even to the point of "humouring the fancies and gratifying the wishes" of such people. For Mother Theresa, all people "personify Christ," such that serving them is to serve Jesus. The work of Christians on behalf of the underprivileged differs from social work precisely in this regard: loving such people is a form of worship for the Christian, whereas from the social work perspective the concern is simply to help people.

Growth in love for God and people is in some respects tied to growth in self-knowledge. On every step of the journey toward love the Christian must seek to understand what motivates them—why they react, respond, hurt, or feel the way that they do. In Paul's words, Christians need to "take captive every thought to make it obedient to Christ" (2 Cor 10:5). Such self-reflective vigilance needs to be present if understanding oneself is a precondition to authentic love. But even such "self-reflective vigilance" needs to be grounded in love, for we can hardly love God and others if we are not at the same time "loving to ourselves."[3] Perhaps somewhat of a corrective to

---

2. Ed. Veronica Zundel, *Eerdman's Book of Famous Prayers* (Grand Rapids: Eerdmans, 1983), 99.

3. I wince both at "self-reflective vigilant" language and "love-for-self" language, for the former has often led to graceless "worm theology" (as, for example, in Thomas à Kempis's classic *Imitation of Christ*) while the latter has often led to narcissistic worship of self—e.g., undue emphases on self-image and inner-healing (as, for example, in

distorting self-knowledge to hatred of self on the one extreme, or worship of self on the other, is the role that community plays in self-knowledge. We can only know ourselves as we are engaged in community with others, for God created us as social beings. Knowing ourselves is therefore directly tied to sharing life in community with others. (At this point I tend to concur with St. Cyprian of Carthage: "You cannot have God as Father unless you have the church as Mother." To be a Christian is to find one's identity in the community of faith, which the New Testament refers to as "the body of Christ." One is only in Christ insofar as one is in his body. Jesus did not teach his disciples to pray "*My* father who is in heaven" but "*Our* father who is in heaven.")

The subjects of love for God and love for neighbor are thus all wrapped up in understanding God's love for us, in serving others, and in knowledge of self—which is, in turn, tied to life in community. The many interconnections between these subjects may be easy enough to understand, but actually loving from the heart and practicing love may be difficult in the extreme. It is for this reason that we might look to the counsel of those who preceded us in the journey of faith. The author of Hebrews exhorted his readers to "run with perseverance the race marked out" for them because they were "surrounded by such a great cloud of witnesses" (Heb 12:1). It is at our own peril that we in the twenty-first century fail to do the same. Nothing is more important than growing in love for God and people. We therefore ought to seize upon any such wisdom that has come from our forebears.

Growing in authentic love for God and people is a lifelong task that will never be perfected on this side of eternity. But knowing a little about the field of spirituality can be of great help along the journey. Where spiritual acuity is absent, theology is cold. If motives behind acts of kindness are without spiritual maturity, such acts may become legalistic. Insofar as ministers and churches are wanting in spiritual life, they can do little more than support the religious establishment. Spirituality is not about being enthusiastic for God. It is not about using our God-given talents for the kingdom. Spiritual success has little to do with church growth, reaching out to the lost, or even the way in which one worships. Spiritual success is counter-intuitive in this respect. Whereas the world cries out "success" when it sees expressions of confidence in the midst of numerical growth, Jesus only cries out "success" when he sees people simply love even though

---

various Evangelical self-help books). I am nevertheless constrained to use such language.

an onslaught of deprivations, insults, crises, and challenges may come their way. Such people are spiritually successful even though they have nothing but hearts filled with love and mercy to show for it. Learning more about love can be of great benefit to all of our endeavors. Evangelicalism would do well, very well indeed, if it focused more on the spiritual life.

Why hasn't Evangelicalism as a whole done so? In this chapter I suggested a few reasons; the principal one is its view that salvation is an event not a process. A related reason is Evangelicalism's fixation on its misunderstanding of justification by faith. This fixation is particularly seen in the typical Evangelical seminarian's understanding of church history, which goes something like this:

> First there was the early church that embraced Paul's teaching of justification by grace through faith. A few centuries later came Constantine, through whom Christianity was legalized. At this point Christianity became Christendom, in which trusting in Jesus Christ as personal Lord and Savior was replaced by organized religion. (Yes, there were also various Christological and Trinitarian arguments that were resolved at this time.) Next follows the Dark Ages or the medieval period in which not much happened. (What is important are those teachings and events from this period that ran counter to the doctrine of justification by grace through faith—e.g., the teaching that the Roman Catholic Church is the mediator between God and humanity.) About one thousand years later (in the sixteenth century) there came the Protestant Reformation when the true Gospel of justification by grace through faith was rediscovered. But alas, Luther and Calvin did not go far enough; and so since their time true Christianity has been trying to return to its biblical roots. Since the eighteenth century, Evangelicalism has single-handedly conveyed the truth of the gospel to the nations.

I trust that I am not here providing a crude or unkind caricature of Evangelical education. While many Evangelical teachers might wince at what I have here said, I am confident that most would be compelled to agree with me. Fixation on the doctrine of justification by grace through faith has blinded Evangelicals to other teachings that are no less important, teachings that thrived in the medieval and post-Reformation periods. We are, indeed, surrounded by a great cloud of witnesses. Throughout the centuries lovers of God in Jesus Christ have emphasized many life-giving teachings that we could profit from if only we would inquire.

Chapter Six

All Truth Is God's Truth

NOT LONG AFTER I became a Christian, I remember a Baptist minister telling me that while other denominations may well be close to the truth, the Baptist faith was best because it was closest to what the Bible says. I did not know what to think of this at the time. Because I did not have the wherewithal to engage the minister in discussion, I simply nodded with consent. But what the minister said did not rest well in me. Sometime in the decade that followed I took a course called "Spiritual Autobiographies" at a Baptist seminary. I enrolled in this course because the course requirements seemed to be relatively light (it was an elective, after all). Little did I know that this course would prove to be the most influential course of my formal education. For the first time in my spiritual journey I paused to reflect on different paradigms of Christian faith. I was pleasantly surprised to find that such paradigms were actually based upon reasonable assumptions, and that there was freshness, authenticity, and vibrancy in them. Some rather judgmental expectations that I had were also dashed—even to the point that the autobiographies that I thought would be most compelling (for they were written by Evangelicals) turned out to be most disappointing. While my subject of choice was Old Testament, the subject that most intrigued me from that time and on has been Christian spirituality. Among many other authors, I grew to love reading St. Augustine, Bernard of Clairvaux, Brother Lawrence of the Resurrection, and more modern authors such as St. Therese of Lisieux and Thomas Merton. I found in them spiritual treasures that were well-nigh absent in Evangelicalism. I saw how some

All Truth Is God's Truth

of them effortlessly unpacked their spiritual journeys with humility and awe. I saw how others longed to abide in Jesus even as they drew nearer to God. I observed how still others saw the kingdom in what is smallest and most mundane. While I did and still do have very real problems with some such authors on various points, on the whole I saw life in them—life which slowly came into me.

The recognition that other expressions of Christian faith may be equally valid as our own naturally leads to the question concerning the degree to which non-Christian religions share in religious truth. This question may be off-putting, even frightening to some; but it is a question that the church must nevertheless address. A central teaching of the historic Christian tradition is that salvation is found only in the person and work of Jesus Christ. While I happily concur with this contention, it seems to me that the Evangelical tradition fails to have a healthy respect for non-Christian faith traditions—for there is no inherent contradiction between believing in the uniqueness of Jesus for salvation and acknowledging that various non-Christian traditions may well have something to say about religious truth.

To begin with, we would do well to ask ourselves the following question: "Is all truth God's truth?" We must, of course, answer yes to this question. Not to do so is to imply that God is somehow finite, even provincial and small. But at the same time answering yes to the question might scare us, for if all truth is God's truth, it follows that we might come across a teaching that is not expressly taught or emphasized in the Christian faith, yet our hearts tell us that the given teaching is nevertheless true.

In order to keep things relatively simple, at this point I will tell you a little about my own story. For the better part of a decade I was most disenchanted with Evangelicalism, not with Jesus, but I repeat, with Evangelicalism. One of my complaints was that I believed that there must be a whole lot more to life in God than what Evangelicalism suggests. Knowing that all truth is God's truth, and knowing that he would keep me in the palm of his hands if I pursued truth outside the Christian faith with all humility, I resolved to study the Scriptures and teachings of other faiths.

For more than ten years now I have studied the teachings of Lao Tzu, a sixth-century BC spiritual teacher from China and the father of Taoism (pronounced "dow-ism"). His teachings have, I believe, helped me to grow as a Christian as they have changed my life in a beautiful manner. At about this same time I also began to study the teachings of Buddhism—particularly

Born Again and Beyond

the Zen variety. As with Taoism, the study and practice of Zen continues to be a life-giving influence in my life. From time to time I also study the Sufi mystics, the Koran, the Bhagavad-Gita and other selections of religious literature. Some have proven to be somewhat or very helpful. Others have had little or no effect on me. Some have even repelled me. If the literature is full of hatred and violence, I have no use for it. If the literature expresses great disregard for the material world and prizes only mental reality, I have little use for it. I celebrate only that which complements the teaching of Jesus. My search is not at all about trying to find a teaching that might compete with the teaching of Jesus, for there is no competition. The teachings of Jesus far surpass any other teachings that I have come across. But this is not to say that teaching from other religions may not complement the teachings of Jesus. All truth is God's truth; and if we are confident enough in believing that Jesus is the Truth, we will have no problem whatever in seeking truth in other religious systems.

In the following paragraphs I will discuss some of the ways in which Taoist and Buddhist teaching has helped me to better understand the teaching of Jesus. I will limit the discussion to Matthew 6:25–34.

> Therefore I tell you, do not worry about your life, what you will eat or drink; or about your body, what you will wear. Is not life more important than food, and the body more important than clothes? Look at the birds of the air; they do not sow or reap or store away in barns, and yet your heavenly Father feeds them. Are you not much more valuable than they? Who of you by worrying can add a single hour to his life? And why do you worry about clothes? See how the lilies of the field grow. They do not labour or spin. Yet I tell you that not even Solomon in all his splendour was dressed like one of these. If that is how God clothes the grass of the field, which is here today and tomorrow is thrown into the fire, will he not much more clothe you, O you of little faith? So do not worry, saying, "What shall we eat?" or "What shall we drink?" or "What shall we wear?" For the pagans run after all these things, and your heavenly Father knows that you need them. But seek first his kingdom and his righteousness, and all these things will be given to you as well. Therefore do not worry about tomorrow, for tomorrow will worry about itself. Each day has enough trouble of its own.

In this celebrated passage Jesus tells us not to worry but to put our trust in the Father who will provide us with all that is necessary. While I bow my heart and mind before Jesus's every word, I nevertheless wish that the gospel recorded more about what Jesus had to say about not worrying. Yes, we must trust God. That's undeniable. But how *does* one trust? Is there anything that one can *do* to make trust easier?

A Christian influenced by Taoism might answer such questions in the following way: "As you seek to be humble you will learn to trust God more easily." Growing in humility in the Taoist tradition is all about seeking to pattern one's heart after the harmony that is observable in creation. For the Taoist, the favorite item within creation in this regard is water. As water seeks the lowest place and there finds rest, so the wise person will seek the lowest place that they might know tranquility. Again, the gentle lapping of water against a boulder slowly erodes the seemingly more powerful boulder even as the water remains unchanged; water similarly finds its way into a tiny fissure in a boulder only to enlarge the fissure and eventually split it. Like water, gentleness and humility are more powerful than might or force. So also, as the Christian seeks to be humble, not clamoring for attention, insisting on their own way, or amassing wealth, the Christian finds greater calm; and when such obstacles as longing for attention and seeking wealth are removed, it becomes easier to trust. There is here no question about religious competition. The Taoist teaching about humility simply complements Jesus's teaching about trust. (There is even something rather Taoist about Jesus's teaching in the given passage, for like Taoism Jesus here invites his hearers to "consider" the birds and the lilies—that is, Jesus counsels them to pattern their lives after what they observe in the created order.) A Christian influenced by Zen might answer the question "How *does* one trust?" in the following way: "Cease to fixate on matters that are beyond your control—what the future holds for you, for example—and you will learn to trust God more fully." A central word in Zen is "attachment." One can be attached to possessions, to past injustices, to possibilities that the future may hold, even to one's own opinions. In order to enjoy tranquility, one needs to let go of all such attachments by simply focusing on the present moment. Zen's great emphases on avoiding attachment and focusing on the present moment is akin to Jesus's teaching not to "worry about tomorrow . . . for each day has enough trouble of its own." Once again, there is no competition; the Zen teaching simply complements the teaching of Jesus.

I trust that my knowledge of and experience with Taoism and Zen Buddhism, while slight, has aided my Christian faith. Like everyone else I struggle with the pride that says "I should be first," and with everyone else I fight against fixating on things that are beyond my control—whether such things be how others think or act, circumstances that affect me, or what the future may hold for me. Without in any way compromising Christian faith, I happily accept legitimate help from anywhere in God's world. I can think of one situation in particular in my life that illustrates how wisdom from the East assisted me. Years ago I traveled to an Anglican retreat center to be interviewed by many individuals over two days. The objective of the interviews was to determine my suitability to ordained ministry in the Anglican Church of Canada. (I was one of about ten others who were being interviewed.) Prior to the beginning of the interviewing process, I went for a long walk in the neighboring forest. I remember sitting on a log and saying to myself such things as "the interviews will go poorly" and "what will I then do?" But before I let such thoughts get the better of me, I reflected on the fact that I was in the hands of God and that I need not concern myself about "tomorrow." I complemented this conviction very naturally by picking up a leaf from the forest floor and studying it. I observed how its coloration varied from shades of yellow to shades of orange; I saw how it was uniquely shaped; and I tried to take in how its central vein fed into smaller veins, which in turn fed into yet smaller veins. I then looked up and saw that the forest floor was covered with millions of such leaves. I believed that God knew the uniqueness of each leaf in the forest and that each leaf was perfectly fulfilling its calling. I then thought of the circumstance that I was in, and I smiled as I reminded myself that God was with me. There is nothing extraordinary about the process that I went through on that fall day to cope with my circumstances. I go through this process regularly, and I know that countless millions of others do so as well. But what if I had never studied the given Eastern traditions? Would I have stepped out of the forest in precisely the same way? I do not think so. I believe that God-given wisdom from the East—wisdom that may be in the Bible as well but is neither emphasized nor expounded upon—did prove to help me at that moment.

So there may well be religious truth outside the Christian faith. A fair question, however, is "is such truth *saving* truth?" That is to say, religious teaching about how to live is not necessarily the same as religious truth concerning salvation. No, I do not believe that truth outside the Christian faith is saving truth. The only saving truth comes through Christ. But this is not really quite fair, for none of the Eastern religions have the same understanding of salvation that Christianity has. Indeed, neither Taoism nor Buddhism have much, or anything to say about the existence of God. The

All Truth Is God's Truth

Judeo-Christian concept of "sin" is equally foreign to Eastern thinking. From a Western perspective, a strong case can be made that Taoism and Buddhism are not even religions as such. They concern, rather, ways of life that lead to inner calm.

The dominant paradigm within Evangelicalism concerning the salvation of people is that there are two groups, the saved and the lost. The saved are those who have been "born again," who have confessed their sins to God, and who have decided to live for Jesus as personal Savior and Lord. The lost are those who have not made such a decision for Jesus, and as a result, have not received forgiveness for their sins, and will be damned to hell for eternity. The lost have failed to make a conscious decision for God for different reasons—perhaps because they have never had the opportunity to do so, perhaps because they grew up in a society that is hostile to the gospel, or perhaps because they have been so battered by representatives of the church that they are unable to hear the message of salvation. These are the damned. Among many others, the following verses are used to support the perspective that Jesus is the only way.

> Salvation is found in no one else, for there is no other name under heaven given to people by which we must be saved. (Acts 4:12)

> For there is one God and one mediator between God and people, the man Christ Jesus. (1 Tim 2:5)

> I am the way and the truth and the life. No one comes to the Father except through me. (John 14:6)

I embrace the fact that there is no salvation outside of Jesus Christ, that he alone is the mediator between God and humanity, and that no one comes to the Father except through him. No, there are not many paths to the top of the mountain. The only path is that provided by Christ. But none of this is to suggest that people cannot know God without first consciously turning to Jesus. Not at all. Jesus is the only way to God, but people don't necessarily have to know this truth consciously before they can experience life in God. Think of the mentally challenged person who knows nothing about Jesus but whose heart is full of mercy. Think of little children (of whom Jesus said, "of such is the kingdom") who almost seem to be programmed to believe—until, of course, they become responsible adults! Think of the scores of people who came into this world before Jesus who nevertheless based their lives on the goodness of God. Think of the millions of people throughout the world who never heard the good news but who nevertheless embraced the values of the kingdom. As with you and me, they too were saved by the blood of Jesus. *There is no reason to privilege conscious knowledge of the means through which God saves humanity over subconscious knowledge that God is merciful.*

Already in the sixteenth century, John Calvin made a distinction between "the visible church" and "the invisible church." By visible church Calvin had in mind those people who were active members of the church, who believed that they had been called by God to live the Christian life through the life of the church. Yet, in Calvin's mind, not all members of the visible church were members of the invisible church, for God alone knows those who have truly been called by him, who confess the faith not to gain the applause of others, but who truly believe in and live the gospel. Akin to Calvin's emphasis on the visible church and the invisible church is the distinction made by more recent theologians between "explicit" and "implicit" Christians. An explicit Christian is someone who is a visible member of the church, who believes in the gospel, who may have been baptized, and who may have made a public profession of faith. An implicit Christian, on the other hand, is one who is likely not a visible member of the church, who may have never even heard the gospel message, and who certainly has not made a public profession of faith. In place of the terminology "implicit Christian," others have spoken of the "anonymous Christian." The anonymous Christian believes in "God" in one way or another. The anonymous Christian also believes that this God is merciful, and that they, too, should therefore live a life of mercy. The truth of God has been written on the anonymous Christian's heart, and while they do not consciously believe in Jesus, it is nevertheless Jesus who has led them to God. The anonymous Christian may be a devout Buddhist monk in the Himalayas, a pious Hindu in India, an old lady prostrating herself before her backyard idols in Africa, or a tribesman from a Pacific island who lived the life of Jesus thousands of years before the first missionaries ever visited the remote island. It is not a proper comprehension of things metaphysical that endears such people to God, but ultimately the crucifixion of Christ—the ongoing influence of which enables anonymous Christians to grow in love and mercy.

A few years ago, while I was a chaplain at an Anglican university, I became friends with a Muslim student. Every Sunday night we would meet in the chapel to discuss religion. While I hoped to convert him even as he hoped to convert me, we had great respect for one another, and we genuinely wished to learn from each other. "Muhammad" would bring his prayer mat along with him, and at nine o'clock he would lay it out and, facing Mecca, pray in Arabic for a few minutes. After one such instance I said to him something like the following, "I believe that God hears your prayers, and that he smiles upon your uprightness. But I also believe that you need to know that you are praying to Jesus." This statement did not seem to be jarring to Muhammad for I had told him many times in the past that Jesus is the embodiment of all virtue, the goal of all authentic religious aspirations, the personal reflection of God himself. I wanted Muhammad to become a Christian so that he could learn to address God as Abba, so that he could have a healthier understanding of mercy, so that he could better reflect in his own life the life of God that was latent in him.

I am only too aware that some might regard this teaching as compromising both the uniqueness of Jesus and the apostolic teaching that salvation is found in Christ alone. But I am not questioning in the least either of these claims. Indeed, I wholeheartedly accept both of them. All that I am saying is that one can experience salvation in Christ without consciously knowing that it is Christ who does the saving. This understanding has proven to be very liberating for me. I no longer view people as either saved or lost. That is God's business, not mine—and not yours. We are called to see the image of God within all people, however broken or sinful they might be. We are called to see the divine spark within all people, even when they themselves do not see it, and we are to ask God to fan that spark into a glowing flame. What Muhammad's eternal state will be, even our own for that matter, is entirely beyond anyone's grasp; and concerning ourselves about it is, dare I say, sinful. If we love God because we fear hell then we do not love God aright. We are then only serving ourselves.

One question that I am regularly confronted with is, "If people do not need to be consciously aware that Jesus is the Savior in order to be saved, what is the purpose of evangelization?" This is a fine question, but perhaps some of the assumptions behind it are problematic. To begin with, we should not obey Jesus only when doing so makes perfect sense to us. More importantly, being saved is as much about embracing the kingdom of heaven now as it is about living in heaven in the hereafter. I don't love Jesus simply because he will save me from eternal flames, but because he has brought me (and continues to bring me) into his kingdom here on earth. Being in the kingdom is reward enough, for the kingdom is the vehicle through which God brings healing to humanity, it is the kingdom that gives us reason and purpose, and being in the kingdom is to anticipate with joy that great wedding banquet.

So why, then, am I a Christian? Some would say that I am only a Christian because Christianity is the dominant religion of North America. I do not dismiss this entirely. But in addition to the fact that I am, to a considerable degree, a product of my own world, I am a Christian because the gospel story has a divine quality about it. It is not something that people could invent. The ethic of Jesus is as brilliant and counter-intuitive as it is life-giving and dumbfounding. The story of the history of salvation from "a wandering Aramean," to the birth of a nation, to a defeated and then victorious messiah, to the birth of the church, and the eventual restoration of all things, smacks of truth. The cause of the restoration of all things—the crucifixion and resurrection of the God-Man Jesus—is altogether wonderful, not something that the early church had the wherewithal to invent, and not something that witnesses of the resurrection would die for were it not true. I could say much more, but doing so would go beyond the confines of this book. Let the following four criteria concerning the validity of any religious truth claim suffice.

- Criterion #1: *For the religious truth claim to be true, it must not regard the individual as the center of all things.* Given the nearly infinite scope of time and space, I simply cannot agree with any worldview that places the individual at the center. I therefore immediately disregard any religious truth claim that includes the manipulation of a deity, spirits, nature, or other people to their own ends. With respect to Christian teaching, there is no question that God (not his creation, not even humanity) is the center of all things. I love what the Psalmist has to say in this regard: "When I consider your heavens, the work of your fingers, the moon and the stars which you have set in place, what is humanity that you are mindful of them?" (Ps 8:3–4). It is partly for this reason that I have little appreciation for "prosperity gospel" teachings, "word of faith" emphases, or anything that resembles them. For it to be true, religion must involve the individual understanding themselves in light of the greatness of the created order.

- Criterion #2: *For the religious truth claim to be true, it must to some degree be founded upon a supra-rational understanding of truth.* This criterion is consistent with the first one insofar as it denies that religious truth can simply be known and defined through human rationality.

All Truth Is God's Truth

Human reason is not the sole arbiter of religious truth. With regard to Christianity, I cherish the emphasis on mystery as well as its holding in tension various truth claims that do not seem to be mutually compatible (e.g., God is three but one; Jesus is God and Man at the same time).

- Criterion #3: *For the religious truth claim to be true, it must have as its focus love—love for self, love for others, and love for God.* In some ways this criterion is but the necessary outworking of the first two criteria. Insofar as the religious truth claim does not emphasize love as its ultimate goal, it is false. I here have great problems with the violence of the Koran. I have similar difficulties with the violence that the Hebrew Bible (Christian Old Testament) advocates in many places. With respect to Christianity, while violence is a very real and sickening part of church history, it is clear that Jesus himself emphasized mercy, forgiveness, turning the other cheek, praying for one's persecutors, and compassion.

- Criterion #4: *For the religious truth claim to be true, it must be holistic.* Religion must integrate heaven and earth, body and soul, and physical reality and mental reality. Insofar as a religious truth claim emphasizes one aspect of existence over the other, its truth value is compromised. I here have great problems with much of Hinduism, for it tends to emphasize mental reality over physical reality. I have an equal problem with monastic and mystical perspectives that focus on the attainment of inner peace without at the same time trying to bring such peace to the world. With regard to Christianity, the belief that God became human is an implicit celebration both of spiritual and physical reality. Jesus's teaching that heaven and earth are united in his kingdom equally suggests this, as does the New Testament teaching that the future is to be experienced and expressed in the present.

One might certainly ask, "what is the basis for such criteria?" My answer is that they are based on nothing else than universal awareness and conscience. I am persuaded that God has placed his truth into the hearts of all humanity, and that while such truth may be distorted, undermined, and challenged in a host of ways, it is nevertheless present in every human heart. Yes, the criteria that I have developed are admittedly Christian sounding. But I do not apologize for this in the least—given that I am myself a Christian, how could the criteria be anything but "Christian sounding"? I do not think that such criteria provide definite reasons for faith. Indeed, I do not think that any reasons whatsoever can provide the stuff of faith. Using reasons to justify faith is akin to trying to explain a sunset to a blind person. In order to know what a sunset is like one has to see it. At best, words can point to what a sunset is like, but words certainly cannot adequately explain a sunset. Religious truth is like this: it can be experienced, but it cannot be reduced to rational explanation. ("What," Tertullian rightly asked, "does Athens have to do with Jerusalem?") The given criteria thus have value only insofar as they *point* to religious truth.

All truth is God's truth; and insofar as one believes that such truth pervades all creation, one can only be inclined to look for it in every setting. No, this does not mean that the Christian should accept all teachings. Not at all. The Christian is, rather, to evaluate all things through the lens of the Word of God—who pierces the darkness with his light.

Conclusion
Evangelicalism on the Edge

MY COMPLAINTS ARE STRICTLY about Evangelicalism, not about Evangelicals themselves. I have dear friends and family members who are Evangelical. I do not think ill of them in the slightest. Indeed, many of them have beautiful faith. People can believe whatever they choose to believe, and by God's grace I hope that I can honor them—for they, too, bear his image. What upsets me is not what people believe or do not believe. It perturbs me when people suggest that they are reflective about faith matters, yet when challenged they retreat to one safe haven or another—the Bible, tradition, or custom. I am also perturbed by any teaching that suggests (or even explicitly teaches) that the Christian faith is only to be thought of along the lines of one system of doctrine or another. Evangelicalism is by no means the only expression of Christian faith that has its bigots, for every expression seems to include those who are unable or unwilling to see life-giving faith in other expressions. Let us learn from one another. Let us freely discuss things with one another in a civil, yet truth-seeking, fashion. And when we think that we have found the truth (or have been found by Truth), let us not then assume the role of prophet and denounce those who fail to see things the way that we do.

Not long ago a well-meaning friend said to me, "I am worried for you because your theology seems to be askew. I can't figure you out." I responded, "Please don't try to figure me out. Just be my friend." I liken this conversation to relationship with God. Those who fixate on doctrine seem to operate from the assumption that friendship with God can only exist upon proper doctrinal grounds. I cannot agree. I told my friend that my relationship with him is not dependent upon knowing his entire life history, the color of his eyes, his body-mass index, and how he relates to others. My relationship with him is all about what we share in common, how we trust one another, and the degree to which we become vulnerable to each other. I think that the same is true with God. Our theologizing and our astuteness in all things doctrinal may have little to do with simple trust in God.

My concern is not so much about erroneous teachings of Evangelicalism, but how such teachings affect the faith of well-meaning Christians who happen to be Evangelical. With regard to loving God, thinking that the Bible is inerrant may not be a problem *per se*; but functionally replacing the authority of God with the authority of a book (inspired though it may be) is most problematic, even idolatrous. Again, thinking that the gospel simply concerns individual salvation may not be a problem *per se*; but failing to be concerned for the rest of God's creation can be a very real problem. Similarly, viewing the cross simply as the means through which Christians are justified without at the same time making the cross central to the daily life of the Christian is foreign to New Testament faith. At every turn of dogma, my concern is not so much with the dogma itself, but how such dogma works itself out in the life of the believer. Evangelicalism has all too often wrongly assumed that understanding the truth and being in the truth are one and the same.

In this book I have challenged Evangelicalism on several fronts. I contended that its understanding of truth is ultimately based on an Enlightenment mindset—a mindset that prizes human rationality above all else. With respect to the Scriptures, I contended that the Evangelical teaching that they are inerrant is little more than the imposition of rational thinking upon the sacred text. As for Evangelicalism's perspective on knowledge, I argued that it leaves insufficient room for the finitude of human knowledge as well as for supra-rational categories such as wonder and mystery. With respect to Evangelicalism's view of doctrine, among other points I contended that its view of doctrinal truth is not consistent with the nature of Scriptural revelation itself—which has come to us mostly in narrative form rather than codified statements. I contended that Evangelicalism's understanding of the evangel is, ironically, most unscriptural—as is its understanding of the cross. As for Evangelicalism's understanding of conversion, I maintained that because it insists on salvation as an event rather than a process, it has failed to address adequately such matters as the relation of

Conclusion

the cross to the Christian life, how the future is to define the present, and growing in love for God and people. In the final chapter I challenged the Evangelical understanding that Christianity alone has a grasp of religious truth. I contended that while Jesus is the only means of eternal salvation, other religious perspectives may nevertheless complement the teaching of Jesus.

All this is not at all to say that Evangelicalism does not have health. Not at all. I think that even given its pronounced weaknesses, Evangelicalism has been a vital force for good in the world. God has used it in advancing his kingdom, in dispelling the darkness, in shaping societies, and in addressing injustices. Perhaps the greatest strength of Evangelicalism concerns its emphasis on the importance of developing a "personal relationship" with God. It seems to me that various churches (including my own) take themselves way too seriously. Some explicitly teach that salvation is mediated through them alone. Others so cloud the gospel with traditions, rites, and the exaltation of clerics that the gospel can scarcely be seen or heard at all. Evangelicalism certainly also has its traditions (the denial that such traditions exist is itself a tradition!). Evangelicalism at times does impede faith (e.g., as it suggests that one can only be in relationship with God if one understands faith in Evangelical categories). But even if it may be inconsistent in this regard, at least in principle it teaches that nothing stands between the individual and God—neither priests, nor sacraments, nor traditions, nor any religious institutions. As I look back at my own journey of faith, and as I have real problems with Evangelicalism in various respects, I nevertheless am happy to express undying gratitude to it for teaching me that God is immediately accessible through Christ.

Another positive feature that I see in Evangelicalism, is, ironically, the ability to divide and separate into different denominations. No doubt, sectarian attitudes within Evangelicalism have legitimately been criticized—for many such divisions have been propelled by pride and the putative desire for doctrinal purity. At one level this is a travesty, for of all groups in society the church should be marked by such virtues as humility and forbearance. But all divisions within Evangelicalism have certainly not arisen from a lack of virtue. Many have arisen for ethnic reasons, geographical reasons, or even missional reasons (e.g., a parachurch organization becoming a denomination in its own right). Moreover, and this is key, in more recent times Evangelicalism has tended to make a distinction between the existence of denominations and denominationalism. For whatever reason, some have presupposed that unity in the Body of Christ is only present where outward, ecclesiastical unity in governance is present. I suppose that this may be a fine goal to strive for—but only insofar as one recognizes that such unity has scarcely ever existed in the real world. The divisions within worldwide Roman Catholicism, Orthodoxy, and Anglicanism (churches that stress visible unity) are no less great than any divisions within Protestantism. (Indeed, there is something rather tragi-comical about different churches contending that real unity will only exist when the others join them—as, for instance, in Vatican II documents!) What is most important is not visible unity but unity in the midst of diversity. Churches must recognize that other churches, that have different roles to play in different parts of this world and that have their own distinctives, are equal members of the Body of Christ. While seeing Christ in mainline Christian traditions is still a great obstacle in the Evangelical mind, particularly since the late twentieth century, Evangelicalism has made great advances in finding unity within itself. Consistent with this, one must be most reticent in castigating the ongoing birth of different Evangelical denominations—for with every such birth the gospel may well be furthered. Even as the gospel forever morphs itself into different worldviews and cultures, so Evangelical denominations come into existence to address different segments of society.

As the years pass, I increasingly learn that I should not take myself too seriously. No, people do not have to think just like I do. No, other attempts to know the truth of God in Jesus Christ are not failed attempts to know the truth as I understand it—or as the Reformed tradition has understood it, or as the Evangelical tradition has understood it. What a relief it has been to be delivered from such sectarianism! As I have stepped back from being dogmatic and looking for certainty, my joy in God has flourished. The more that I remind myself that I am altogether common, the more I enjoy life in God. I encourage Evangelical leaders to do the same with regard to their religious culture. I suspect that as Evangelicalism grows to appreciate its folkish nature, and the less it takes itself too seriously, the more it will fulfill its God-given role in the kingdom.

www.ingramcontent.com/pod-product-compliance
Lightning Source LLC
Chambersburg PA
CBHW020857160426
43192CB00007B/958